Mastering OAuth 2.0

Create powerful applications to interact with popular service providers such as Facebook, Google, Twitter, and more by leveraging the OAuth 2.0 Authorization Framework

Charles Bihis

[PACKT] open source*
PUBLISHING   community experience distilled

BIRMINGHAM - MUMBAI

Mastering OAuth 2.0

Copyright © 2015 Packt Publishing

All rights reserved. No part of this book may be reproduced, stored in a retrieval system, or transmitted in any form or by any means, without the prior written permission of the publisher, except in the case of brief quotations embedded in critical articles or reviews.

Every effort has been made in the preparation of this book to ensure the accuracy of the information presented. However, the information contained in this book is sold without warranty, either express or implied. Neither the author, nor Packt Publishing, and its dealers and distributors will be held liable for any damages caused or alleged to be caused directly or indirectly by this book.

Packt Publishing has endeavored to provide trademark information about all of the companies and products mentioned in this book by the appropriate use of capitals. However, Packt Publishing cannot guarantee the accuracy of this information.

First published: December 2015

Production reference: 1081215

Published by Packt Publishing Ltd.
Livery Place
35 Livery Street
Birmingham B3 2PB, UK.

ISBN 978-1-78439-540-7

www.packtpub.com

Credits

Author
Charles Bihis

Reviewers
Shubham Jindal
Oleg Mikheev

Commissioning Editor
Pramila Balan

Acquisition Editors
Richard Harvey
Aaron Lazar

Content Development Editor
Rohit Singh

Technical Editor
Siddhi Rane

Copy Editors
Janbal Dharmaraj
Kevin McGowan

Project Coordinator
Mary Alex

Proofreader
Safis Editing

Indexer
Priya Sane

Graphics
Kirk D'Penha

Production Coordinator
Komal Ramchandani

Cover Work
Komal Ramchandani

About the Author

Charles Bihis is a scientist and engineer from Vancouver, Canada. Earning his degree in computer science from the University of British Columbia, specializing in software engineering, he enjoys exploring the boundaries of technology. He believes that technology is the key to enriching the lives of everyone around us and strives to solve problems people face every day. Reach out to him on his website, www.whoischarles.com, and let's solve the world's problems together!

> This work would not have been possible without the help of my colleagues, friends, and family. A special thanks goes to my teammates on the Identity Platform team at Adobe for the years of guidance and tutelage. I'd also like to thank my friends for their constant support and encouragement. And finally, I'd like to thank my family, especially my wife, for their ceaseless confidence in all that I do.

About the Reviewers

Shubham Jindal has an avid interest in programming and is currently pursuing his degree in computer science and engineering from Indian Institute of Technology, Delhi. Leaning towards JavaScript, he breathes computers and can be easily spotted hacking around with things, scripting or inspecting elements on the Web. Being a clinophile, he believes in doing smart work. Inclined towards music since childhood, you can inevitably find him with his earphones plugged in.

He is always agog for new opportunities and is striving to establish his very own start-up.

> I would like to thank Dr. Karthikeyan Bhargavan—my INRIA's internship mentor, parents, friends, and Vartika Garg—my partner in crime, for their help in producing this book.

Oleg Mikheev is a computer science enthusiast with over 17 years background both in industry and academia, holding a PhD from one of the top Russian universities. He has completed numerous projects in industries where security is always a top priority—finance, insurance, government.

The list of clients Oleg has worked for includes names such as UBS, CSFB and NYSE, where he has applied a full stack of technologies, specifically IBM WebSphere. Lately, Oleg is focused on start-up ventures, currently working in a financial start-up, Personal Capital.

He has authored a number of articles for the Java World journal, contributed to open source projects and reviewed a book on Struts 2.

> I would like to thank Mary Alex for her exceptional work and would like to wish her the best of luck with her married life.

www.PacktPub.com

Support files, eBooks, discount offers, and more

For support files and downloads related to your book, please visit www.PacktPub.com.

Did you know that Packt offers eBook versions of every book published, with PDF and ePub files available? You can upgrade to the eBook version at www.PacktPub.com and as a print book customer, you are entitled to a discount on the eBook copy. Get in touch with us at service@packtpub.com for more details.

At www.PacktPub.com, you can also read a collection of free technical articles, sign up for a range of free newsletters and receive exclusive discounts and offers on Packt books and eBooks.

https://www2.packtpub.com/books/subscription/packtlib

Do you need instant solutions to your IT questions? PacktLib is Packt's online digital book library. Here, you can search, access, and read Packt's entire library of books.

Why subscribe?

- Fully searchable across every book published by Packt
- Copy and paste, print, and bookmark content
- On demand and accessible via a web browser

Free access for Packt account holders

If you have an account with Packt at www.PacktPub.com, you can use this to access PacktLib today and view 9 entirely free books. Simply use your login credentials for immediate access.

To my wife, Stephanie, my mom, Purificacion, and my aunt, Elizabeth, the three most important women in my life. Everything I do is possible because of you.

-Charles

Table of Contents

Preface	**ix**
Chapter 1: Why Should I Care About OAuth 2.0?	**1**
Authentication versus authorization	**2**
Authentication	2
Authorization	2
What problems does it solve?	**3**
Federated identity	3
Delegated authority	4
Real-life examples of OAuth 2.0 in action	4
How does OAuth 2.0 actually solve the problem?	**5**
Without OAuth 2.0 – GoodApp wants to suggest contacts by looking at your Facebook friends	5
With OAuth 2.0 – GoodApp wants to suggest contacts by looking at your Facebook friends	7
Who uses OAuth 2.0?	**8**
Introducing "The World's Most Interesting Infographic Generator"	**9**
Summary	**9**
Chapter 2: A Bird's Eye View of OAuth 2.0	**11**
How does it work?	**11**
User consent	13
Two main flows for two main types of client	16
Trusted versus untrusted clients	17
First look at the client-side flow	**18**
An untrusted client – GoodApp requests access for user's Facebook friends using implicit grant	19
The big picture	21
When should this be used?	22
Pros and cons of being an untrusted client	22

Pros	23
Cons	23
First look at the server-side flow	**23**
A trusted client – GoodApp requests access for user's Facebook friends using authorization code grant	24
The big picture	26
When should this be used?	28
Pros and cons of being a trusted client	29
Pros	29
Cons	29
What are the differences?	**29**
What about mobile?	**30**
Summary	**31**
Chapter 3: Four Easy Steps	**33**
Let's get started	**33**
Step 1 – Register your client application	**35**
Different service providers, different registration process, same OAuth 2.0 protocol	36
Your client credentials	38
Step 2 – Get your access token	**38**
A closer look at access tokens	39
Scope	39
Duration of access	41
Token revocation	41
Sometimes a refresh token	42
Step 3 – Use your access token	**42**
An access token is an access token	43
Step 4 – Refresh your access token	**43**
What if I don't have a refresh token?	43
Refresh tokens expire too	43
Putting it all together	**44**
Summary	**44**
Chapter 4: Register Your Application	**45**
Recap of registration process	**45**
Registering your application with Facebook	**46**
Creating your application	46
Setting your redirection endpoint	48
What is a redirection endpoint?	48
Find your service provider's authorization and token endpoints	53
Putting it all together!	**53**
Summary	**54**

Chapter 5: Get an Access Token with the Client-Side Flow   55
Refresher on the implicit grant flow   55
A closer look at the implicit grant flow   57
Authorization request   58
- According to the specification   58
- In our application   59
Access token response   60
- Success   60
- Error   62
Let's build it!   63
Build the base application   64
- Install Apache Maven   64
- Create the project   66
- Configure base project to fit our application   67
- Modify the hosts file   68
- Running it for the first time   68
Make the authorization request   71
Handle the access token response   73
Summary   77
Reference pages   78
Authorization request   79
Access token response   80
Error response   80

Chapter 6: Get an Access Token with the Server-Side Flow   83
Refresher on the authorization code grant flow   83
A closer look at the authorization code grant flow   86
Authorization request   86
- According to the specification   86
- In our application   87
Authorization response   88
- Success   88
- Error   89
Access token request   91
- According to the specification   91
- In our application   93
Access token response   94
- Success   94
- Error   95
Let's build it!   96
Build the base application   96
- Install Apache Maven   96
- Create the project   97
- Configure the base project to fit our application   99
- Modify the hosts file   100

Table of Contents

    Running it for the first time   100
  Make the authorization request   102
  Handle the authorization response   104
  Make the access token request   106
  Handle the access token response   108
Summary   **111**
Reference pages   **112**
  An overview of the authorization code grant flow   112
  Authorization request   113
  Authorization response   114
  Error response   114
  Access token request   115
  Access token response   116
  Error response   117

Chapter 7: Use Your Access Token   119

Refresher on access tokens   **119**
Use your access token to make an API call   **120**
  The authorization request header field   120
  The form-encoded body parameter   121
  The URI query parameter   121
Let's build it!   **122**
  In our client-side application   123
    Send via the URI query parameter   124
    Send via the form-encoded body parameter   125
  In our server-side application   126
    Send via the URI query parameter   126
    Send via the HTTP authorization header   128
Creating the world's most interesting infographic   **130**
Summary   **130**
Reference pages   **131**
  An overview of protected resource access   131
  The authorization request header field   132
  The form-encoded body parameter   132
  The URI query parameter   133

Chapter 8: Refresh Your Access Token   135

A closer look at the refresh token flow   **135**
  The refresh request   136
    According to the specification   136
  The access token response   137
    Success   137
    Error   138

What if I have no refresh token? Or my refresh token has expired?	**139**
Comparison between the two methods	140
The ideal workflow	**141**
Summary	**142**
Reference pages	**143**
An overview of the refresh token flow	143
The refresh request	144
Access token response	144
Error response	145
Chapter 9: Security Considerations	**147**
What's at stake?	**147**
Security best practices	**148**
Use TLS!	148
Request minimal scopes	149
When using the implicit grant flow, request read-only permissions	149
Keep credentials and tokens out of reach of users	150
Use the authorization code grant flow whenever possible	150
Use the refresh token whenever possible	151
Use native browsers instead of embedded browsers	151
Do not use third-party scripts in the redirection endpoint	153
Rotate your client credentials	154
Common attacks	**154**
Cross-site request forgery (CSRF)	154
What's going on?	156
Use the state param to combat CSRF	156
Phishing	158
Redirection URI manipulation	160
Client and user impersonation	162
Summary	**162**
Chapter 10: What About Mobile?	**163**
What is a mobile application?	**163**
What flow should we use for mobile applications?	**164**
Are mobile applications trusted or untrusted?	164
What about mobile applications built on top of mobile platforms with secure storage APIs?	165
Not quite enough	165
Hybrid architectures	**167**
Implicit for mobile app, authorization code grant for backend server	168
What is the benefit of this?	169
Authorization via application instead of user-agent	**169**
Summary	**171**

Chapter 11: Tooling and Troubleshooting — 173
Tools — 173
Troubleshooting — 174
The implicit grant flow — 174
The authorization request — 174
The authorization code grant flow — 177
The authorization request — 177
The access token request — 178
The API call flow — 179
The authorization request header field — 179
The form-encoded body parameter — 180
The URI query parameter — 181
The refresh token flow — 182
Summary — 183
Chapter 12: Extensions to OAuth 2.0 — 185
Extensions to the OAuth 2.0 framework — 185
Custom grant types — 185
A variety of token types — 186
Any authorization backend — 187
OpenID Connect — 187
Summary — 189
Appendix A: Resource Owner Password Credentials Grant — 191
When should you use it? — 191
Reference pages — 192
An overview of the resource owner password credentials grant — 192
Authorization request and response — 193
Access token request — 193
Access token response — 194
Error response — 194
Appendix B: Client Credentials Grant — 197
When should you use it? — 197
Reference pages — 198
Overview of the client credentials grant — 198
Authorization request and response — 198
Access token request — 198
Access token response — 199
Error response — 200

Appendix C: Reference Specifications — 201
The OAuth 2 Authorization Framework — 201
The OAuth 2 Authorization Framework: Bearer Token Usage — 201
OAuth 2.0 Token Revocation — 201
OAuth 2.0 Thread Model and Security Considerations — 202
Security Assertion Markup Language (SAML) 2.0 Profile for OAuth 2.0 Client Authentication and Authorization Grants — 202
JSON Web Token (JWT) — 202
JSON Web Token (JWT) Profile for OAuth 2.0 Client Authentication and Authorization Grants — 203
OpenID Connect Core 1.0 — 203
Index — 205

Preface

The Internet is a thriving and dynamic ecosystem. Living and playing within this ecosystem are many world-class services, all offering world-class technologies. Think about the massive social graph that Facebook hosts, the most up-to-date mapping system proudly owned and operated by Google, or the ever-growing professional network that is available from LinkedIn. All of these companies, and more, are presenting their world-class technologies for the world to use!

Until recently, it was very difficult to access these technologies in your own applications. Each company would create their own protocols for how to access and leverage their respective technologies. You may have heard of Yahoo!'s BBAuth, or Google's AuthSub. These are just a couple of examples of proprietary protocols created to allow people to leverage these company's services. Unfortunately, the trend of creating and using proprietary protocols just doesn't scale. Enter OAuth 2.0.

OAuth 2.0 is an open protocol for delegating authorization to such services, and it has become the standard authorization protocol used by companies around the world. It allows developers like you and I to access these world-class technologies and use them in our own applications! It is a fascinating problem space with an equally fascinating and elegant solution.

I've been lucky enough to work in the Identity space for the past 7 years, and during this time, I've been able to witness the evolution and progression of this protocol. *Mastering OAuth 2.0* is an attempt at distilling the most important parts of the protocol, including design and usage. With a hard focus on practicality and security, this book focuses on the parts of integration that will give application developers like you and I the most benefit and mileage.

As OAuth 2.0 continues to gain adoption, and more and more services become available for developers to integrate with and leverage, I'm hoping that this book will allow you to be able to comfortably dive in and start building the next generation of world-class applications and technologies!

What this book covers

Chapter 1, Why Should I Care About OAuth 2.0?, introduces the OAuth 2.0 protocol, and discusses its purpose, prevalence, and importance.

Chapter 2, A Bird's Eye View of OAuth 2.0, takes a high-level look at the OAuth 2.0 protocol and the different workflows it describes.

Chapter 3, Four Easy Steps, enumerates the simple steps necessary to integrate with a service provider using the OAuth 2.0 protocol.

Chapter 4, Register Your Application, details the first of these four steps which covers registering your application with the service provider.

Chapter 5, Get an Access Token with the Client-Side Flow, discusses the complicated topic of gaining access to a protected resource from what we call an untrusted client.

Chapter 6, Get an Access Token with the Server-Side Flow, discusses the complicated topic of gaining access to a protected resource from what we call a trusted client.

Chapter 7, Use Your Access Token, outlines the process for exercising access to a resource once it has been granted to you.

Chapter 8, Refresh Your Access Token, talks about the process of refreshing your access once it expires.

Chapter 9, Security Considerations, discusses the many important security considerations to be made in your application. This is an important topic for any application, but is especially important given the power that this protocol allows.

Chapter 10, What About Mobile?, is a chapter dedicated to the topic of mobile devices, including phones and tablets, and all of the considerations that come with it.

Chapter 11, Tooling and Troubleshooting, talks about how to troubleshoot issues with your integration as well as how to appropriately handle errors so as to minimize user interaction.

Chapter 12, Extensions to OAuth 2.0, looks at the various ways OAuth 2.0 can be extended to satisfy a multitude of use cases.

Appendix A, Resource Owner Password Credentials Grant, takes a look at one of the supplemental supported flows in the book.

Appendix B, Client Credentials Grant, takes a look at another of the supplemental supported flows in the book.

Appendix C, Reference Specifications, enumerates the various open specifications that are referenced throughout the book.

What you need for this book

To create the sample applications described in this book, you will need Java 8, Apache Maven 3, a modern web browser (such as Google Chrome, Microsoft Edge, or Mozilla Firefox), and a text editor of your choice. Several libraries and command-line utilities will be utilized as well, including JQuery, Apache HTTPClient, and cURL. A basic understanding of programming and OAuth is recommended.

Who this book is for

This book is written for application developers, software architects, security engineers, and casual programmers alike, looking to leverage the power of OAuth 2.0 in their own services and applications. It covers basic topics such as registering your application and choosing an appropriate workflow, and advanced topics such as security considerations and extensions to the specification. This book has something for everyone.

Conventions

In this book, you will find a number of text styles that distinguish between different kinds of information. Here are some examples of these styles and an explanation of their meaning.

Code words in text, database table names, folder names, filenames, file extensions, pathnames, dummy URLs, user input, and Twitter handles are shown as follows: "Open up your favorite HTML editor and create a new file, index.html, place it where index.jsp was."

A block of code is set as follows:

```
function makeRequest() {
  // Define properties
  var AUTH_ENDPOINT = "https://www.facebook.com/dialog/oauth";
  var RESPONSE_TYPE = "token";
  var CLIENT_ID = "wmiig-550106";
  var REDIRECT_URI = "http://wmiig.com/callback.html";
  var SCOPE = "public_profile user_posts";
```

Any command-line input or output is written as follows:

```
sudo mvn -Dmaven.tomcat.port=80 -Dmaven.tomcat.path=/ tomcat:run
```

New terms and **important words** are shown in bold. Words that you see on the screen, for example, in menus or dialog boxes, appear in the text like this: "Save the file, reload your page, and click on **Go!** again."

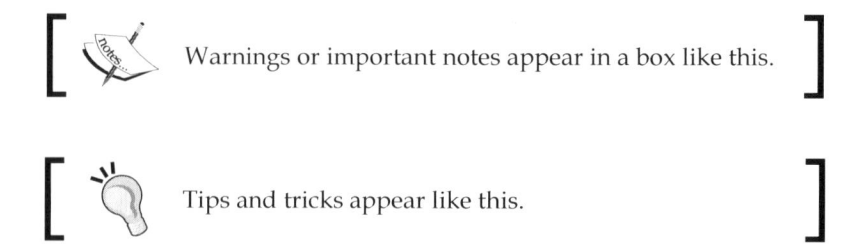

> Warnings or important notes appear in a box like this.

> Tips and tricks appear like this.

Reader feedback

Feedback from our readers is always welcome. Let us know what you think about this book—what you liked or disliked. Reader feedback is important for us as it helps us develop titles that you will really get the most out of.

To send us general feedback, simply e-mail `feedback@packtpub.com`, and mention the book's title in the subject of your message.

If there is a topic that you have expertise in and you are interested in either writing or contributing to a book, see our author guide at `www.packtpub.com/authors`.

Customer support

Now that you are the proud owner of a Packt book, we have a number of things to help you to get the most from your purchase.

Downloading the example code

You can download the example code files from your account at `http://www.packtpub.com` for all the Packt Publishing books you have purchased. If you purchased this book elsewhere, you can visit `http://www.packtpub.com/support` and register to have the files e-mailed directly to you.

Errata

Although we have taken every care to ensure the accuracy of our content, mistakes do happen. If you find a mistake in one of our books—maybe a mistake in the text or the code—we would be grateful if you could report this to us. By doing so, you can save other readers from frustration and help us improve subsequent versions of this book. If you find any errata, please report them by visiting `http://www.packtpub.com/submit-errata`, selecting your book, clicking on the **Errata Submission Form** link, and entering the details of your errata. Once your errata are verified, your submission will be accepted and the errata will be uploaded to our website or added to any list of existing errata under the Errata section of that title.

To view the previously submitted errata, go to `https://www.packtpub.com/books/content/support` and enter the name of the book in the search field. The required information will appear under the **Errata** section.

Piracy

Piracy of copyrighted material on the Internet is an ongoing problem across all media. At Packt, we take the protection of our copyright and licenses very seriously. If you come across any illegal copies of our works in any form on the Internet, please provide us with the location address or website name immediately so that we can pursue a remedy.

Please contact us at `copyright@packtpub.com` with a link to the suspected pirated material.

We appreciate your help in protecting our authors and our ability to bring you valuable content.

Questions

If you have a problem with any aspect of this book, you can contact us at `questions@packtpub.com`, and we will do our best to address the problem.

1
Why Should I Care About OAuth 2.0?

As an application developer, you may have heard the term OAuth 2.0 thrown around a lot. OAuth 2.0 has gained wide adoption by web service and software companies around the world, and is integral to the way these companies interact and share information. But what exactly is it? In a nutshell…

OAuth 2.0 is a protocol that allows distinct parties to share information and resources in a secure and reliable manner.

This is the major tenet of the OAuth 2.0 protocol, which we will spend the rest of the book learning about and utilizing. Also, in this chapter, we will introduce the sample application that we will be building throughout this book, *The World's Most Interesting Infographic Generator*.

> **What about OAuth 1.0?**
>
> Built with the same motivation, OAuth 1.0 was designed and ratified in 2007. However, it was criticized for being overly complex and also had issues with imprecise specifications, which led to insecure implementations. All of these issues contributed to poor adoption for OAuth 1.0, and eventually led to the design and creation of OAuth 2.0. OAuth 2.0 is the successor to OAuth 1.0.
>
> It is also important to note that OAuth 2.0 is not backwards compatible with OAuth 1.0, and so OAuth 2.0 applications cannot integrate with OAuth 1.0 service providers.

Authentication versus authorization

Before we dive into our discussion of OAuth 2.0, it is important to first define some terms. There are two terms in particular that are pivotal to our understanding of OAuth 2.0 and its uses: **authentication** and **authorization**. These terms are often conflated and sometimes interchanged, but they actually represent two distinct concepts, and their distinction is important to understand before continuing our discussion of OAuth 2.0.

Authentication

Authentication is the process of validating whether a person (or system) is actually who they say they are.

An example of this is when you go to the bank to withdraw money, and you provide your bank card and PIN to the teller. In some cases, the teller may ask for additional identification, such as your driver's license, to verify your identity. You may recognize this in other instances when you provide your username and password to a website, say, to view a document.

Authorization

Authorization is the process of determining what actions you are allowed to perform once you have been authenticated.

Referring to our previous bank example, once the teller has verified who you are, they can then proceed to fulfill your request to withdraw money. In order to do this, they must check whether you are allowed to withdraw money from the account that you are requesting (that is, you are actually the owner of the account). Relating to our website example, once you have authenticated by providing your username and password, the website will then check to see whether you are indeed allowed to see the document that you are requesting. This is usually done by looking up your permissions in some access control list.

Now that we have established the distinction between these two important concepts, we can look at what OAuth 2.0 actually is and the problems it solves.

What problems does it solve?

Have you ever logged into a site using your Google account? Have you ever posted to Pinterest and Instagram at the same time? Have you ever shared a link to your wall from any application other than Facebook? These are all examples of OAuth 2.0 in use!

At a high level, the OAuth 2.0 protocol allows two parties to exchange information securely and reliably. In more practical terms, you'll find that the most common uses of OAuth 2.0 involve two things:

- Allowing a user to log into an application with another account. For example, Pinterest allowing users to log in with their Twitter accounts. This is known as **federated identity**.
- Allowing one service to access resources on another service on behalf of the user. For example, Adobe accessing your Facebook photos on your behalf. This is known as **delegated authority**.

Both of these combine to allow the creation of powerful applications that can all integrate with each other.

> Both of the scenarios mentioned in the preceding list are actually really the same scenario. In both, the user is accessing a protected resource on behalf of another party. In the first example, the protected resource is the user's account information, while in the second example the protected resource is the user's Facebook photos. This will become clearer as we explore the details of how the OAuth 2.0 protocol handles these situations.

Federated identity

Federated identity is an important concept in identity management. It refers to the concept that allows one service provider to allow authentication of a user using their identity with another service provider. For instance, imagine a user that logs into Foursquare and Amazon with their Facebook credentials. In this example, the user only needs to maintain a single user account, their Facebook account, which gives them access to several service providers; in this case, Facebook itself, plus Foursquare, and Amazon. They don't need to create individual accounts on Foursquare or Amazon, and therefore, don't need to maintain three separate passwords. In this sense, the user's identities across these sites are federated, as in, they are made to act as one.

> **The OAuth 2.0 Authorization Framework**
>
> Strictly speaking, the OAuth 2.0 protocol is actually an authorization protocol and not an authentication protocol. Because of this, OAuth 2.0 alone cannot provide federated identity. However, when used in a certain way, and in conjunction with other protocols, OAuth 2.0 can provide federated authentication, which is a key component to federated identity systems.
>
> See the *OpenID Connect* section in *Chapter 12*, *Extensions to OAuth 2.0*, to see how the OAuth 2.0 protocol can be combined with OpenID to provide an authentication layer on top of the authorization framework described by the OAuth 2.0 specification.

Delegated authority

Delegated authority is another important concept in the identity space. It refers to the ability for a service or application to gain access to a user's resources on their behalf. Take, for instance, LinkedIn, which can suggest contacts for you to add by looking at your Google contact list. In this example, LinkedIn will be able to view your Google contact list on your behalf. Permission to access your Google contacts has been delegated to LinkedIn.

Real-life examples of OAuth 2.0 in action

Now that we understand the basic principles of OAuth 2.0, let's take a look at some everyday, real-life examples of OAuth 2.0 in action:

- StackOverflow allowing you to log in with your Google account
- Posting a status update from your phone using the Facebook mobile application
- LinkedIn suggesting contacts for you to add by looking at your Google contacts
- Pinterest allowing you to pin something from a WordPress blog
- Sharing an article to your Facebook feed from the article itself

As you can see, if you've ever done any of these things, or anything similar, you have probably already used OAuth 2.0.

How does OAuth 2.0 actually solve the problem?

In order to see how OAuth 2.0 solves this problem of sharing resources, let's look at how this problem was solved before OAuth 2.0 was created.

Without OAuth 2.0 – GoodApp wants to suggest contacts by looking at your Facebook friends

Imagine that you have just signed up for the service GoodApp. As a new user, you don't have any contacts. GoodApp wants to suggest contacts for you to add by looking at your Facebook friends. If any of your Facebook friends are on GoodApp, it will suggest that you add them.

Before the creation of OAuth 2.0, this was solved in a very insecure way. GoodApp would ask you for your username and password for Facebook. GoodApp would then log into Facebook on your behalf to get your friends. This interaction can be looked at like this:

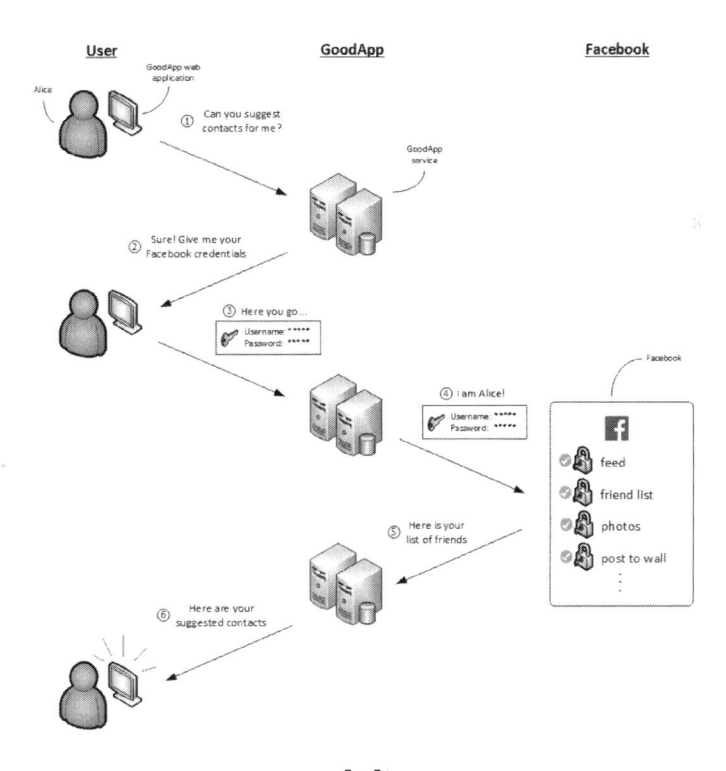

Here is how it works:

1. You ask GoodApp to suggest contacts to you.
2. GoodApp responds by saying, "Sure! Just give me your Facebook username and password please!"
3. You give GoodApp your username and password for your Facebook account.
4. GoodApp then logs into Facebook using your credentials, effectively impersonating you, to request your friend list.
5. Facebook happily obliges, giving GoodApp your friend list.
6. GoodApp then uses this information to tailor suggested contacts for you.

Why is this a bad idea? There are five key reasons:

- **You have given GoodApp the power to do *anything* with your account**: This is known proverbially as giving it the "keys to the city". You have essentially given GoodApp access to everything in your account, as if they were you. Now imagine it wasn't GoodApp. Instead it was NewUnknownApp. It's easy to see how this becomes very dangerous.

- **GoodApp may save your password, and may do so insecurely**: In order for GoodApp to maintain access to your account, they would need to store your credentials. The act of storing your password is an extremely bad practice and should be avoided at all times. To make things worse, different companies enforce different standards of security, some of which are shockingly low.

- **You are giving more chances for your password to get stolen**: You are sending your username and password across the Internet. The more times you do this, the more risk there is for someone to steal it.

- **You have to change your Facebook password if GoodApp ever gets hacked**: If GoodApp somehow got compromised, your Facebook credentials will also have been compromised. You would then need to change your Facebook password as a result of GoodApp getting owned.

- **There is no way to revoke access**: If GoodApp was acquired by EvilCorp and started doing things that you didn't like, the only way to revoke access would be to change your Facebook credentials.

With OAuth 2.0 – GoodApp wants to suggest contacts by looking at your Facebook friends

Now, let's take a look at that interaction, but this time utilizing the OAuth 2.0 protocol. In this scenario, GoodApp would "ask" Facebook for your friend list. You give permission to this by logging into Facebook and approving the request. Once the request is approved, GoodApp would then be able to fetch your friend list from Facebook on your behalf.

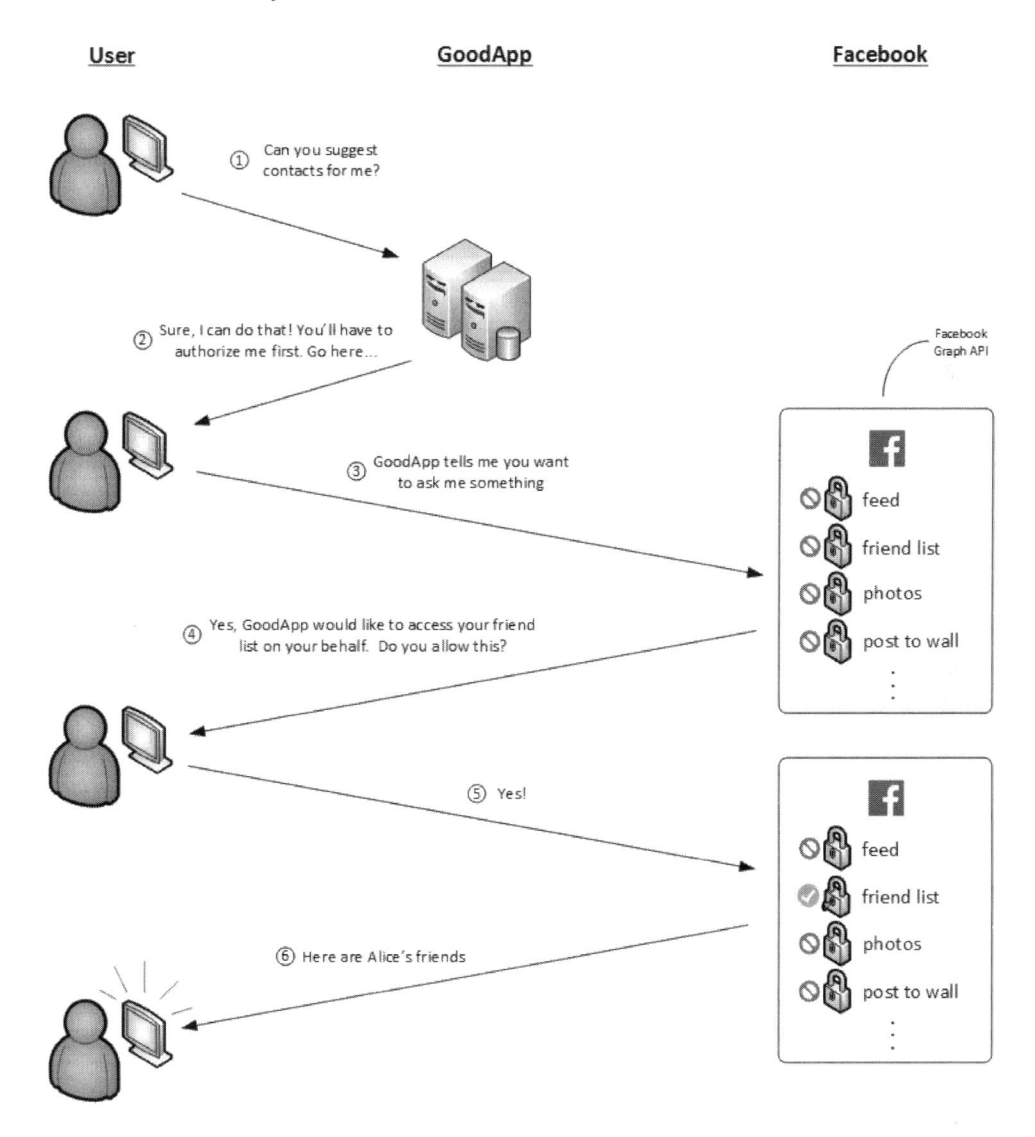

User   **GoodApp**   **Facebook**

① Can you suggest contacts for me?

② Sure, I can do that! You'll have to authorize me first. Go here...

Facebook Graph API

③ GoodApp tells me you want to ask me something

- ⊘ feed
- ⊘ friend list
- ⊘ photos
- ⊘ post to wall

④ Yes, GoodApp would like to access your friend list on your behalf. Do you allow this?

⑤ Yes!

- ⊘ feed
- ✓ friend list
- ⊘ photos
- ⊘ post to wall

⑥ Here are Alice's friends

Let's have a look at the flow:

1. You ask GoodApp to suggest contacts to you.
2. GoodApp says, "Sure! But you'll have to authorize me first. Go here…"
3. GoodApp sends you to Facebook to log in and authorize GoodApp.
4. Facebook asks you directly for authorization to see if GoodApp can access your friend list on your behalf.
5. You say "yes".
6. Facebook happily obliges, giving GoodApp your friend list. GoodApp then uses this information to tailor suggested contacts for you.

Why is this better? Five key reasons to contrast the five points in the previous example:

- **You aren't giving it the "keys to the city" anymore**: Notice, in this example, you aren't giving your Facebook username and password to GoodApp. Instead, you are giving it directly to Facebook. Now, GoodApp doesn't have to even worry about your Facebook credentials.
- **Since you aren't giving your credentials, GoodApp no longer needs to store them**: With your authority delegated from Facebook, you don't need to worry that GoodApp is storing, or even seeing, your Facebook password.
- **You send your password across the Internet less frequently**: If you already had an active session with Facebook, you actually wouldn't need to reauthenticate with them. If GoodApp has federated identities with Facebook, you would have to send your password even less frequently.
- **You don't have to change your Facebook password if GoodApp ever gets hacked**: This is because of the next point.
- **There is a way to revoke access**: OAuth 2.0 provides the ability for a service provider to revoke access to a client. If GoodApp ever got compromised, or got acquired by Evil Corp, you could go to Facebook and revoke GoodApp's access.

Who uses OAuth 2.0?

In the previous section, we mentioned that OAuth 2.0 has become one of the most important protocols for applications and service providers today. But how important is it? Here is a short, non-exhaustive list of some of the biggest supporters of the OAuth 2.0 protocol, along with some of the capabilities that they provide:

- **Google**: You can leverage a multitude of Google's services by interacting with their APIs via OAuth 2.0

- **Facebook**: Facebook's social graph is accessed via OAuth 2.0 and allows users to do a tremendous amount of things, including posting to their wall and sending messages
- **Instagram**: Instagram allows you to access a user's feed and post comments and likes
- **LinkedIn**: Post comments, share links, and gather engagement statistics via the LinkedIn APIs
- **Spotify**: Query Spotify's massive music catalog and manage user's playlists using Spotify's APIs
- **Foursquare**: The Foursquare API lets you look up users and places from all over the world

There are many, many more companies that use and support the OAuth 2.0 protocol. This gives developers an enormous amount of power to create amazing applications that can leverage all of these world-class services.

Introducing "The World's Most Interesting Infographic Generator"

The best way to learn is simply by doing it. So, to learn the concepts of OAuth 2.0, we will be building an application throughout this book that will integrate with Facebook. It will be called *The World's Most Interesting Infographic Generator*. It will allow a user to log in with their Facebook account, request their profile data and a list of their most recent posts, and return interesting statistics about their posting habits. You can see a working example of this application at www.worldsmostinterestinginfographic.com, or www.wmiig.com for short.

Summary

In this chapter, we took an introductory look at what OAuth 2.0 is and how it is used all around us. We discussed the benefits that this protocol gives us and even looked at the kind of adoption that has taken place in the industry. It has become one of the most, if not the most, used and adopted authorization protocols on the Internet due, in large part, to the power that it gives application developers, start-ups, and corporations alike, to share information.

In the next chapter, we will look at how OAuth 2.0 provides these benefits by looking at how OAuth 2.0 actually works under the hood. Get ready!

A Bird's Eye View of OAuth 2.0

In the previous chapter, we talked about what OAuth 2.0 is and its importance in today's technology industry. We established that the protocol is used to effectively exchange information and resources between parties to serve a multitude of purposes (remember federated identity and delegated authority?). But how does it actually achieve these things? This is what we will explore next.

In this chapter, we will take a look at how OAuth 2.0 works at a high level. We will use this knowledge to explore and understand the various ways in which it is used, from websites to mobile devices to desktop applications, and the differences in each.

How does it work?

Let's revisit our example scenario. You have just signed up for the service GoodApp, and now GoodApp would like to suggest contacts for you to add by looking at your Facebook friends. In the last chapter, we looked at the old model, where GoodApp would ask you for your username and password and use them to access your Facebook friend list on your behalf. We then looked at the new, superior model that uses OAuth 2.0 to achieve the same thing, but in a much more secure and manageable way.

A Bird's Eye View of OAuth 2.0

The (simplified) workflow looks like this:

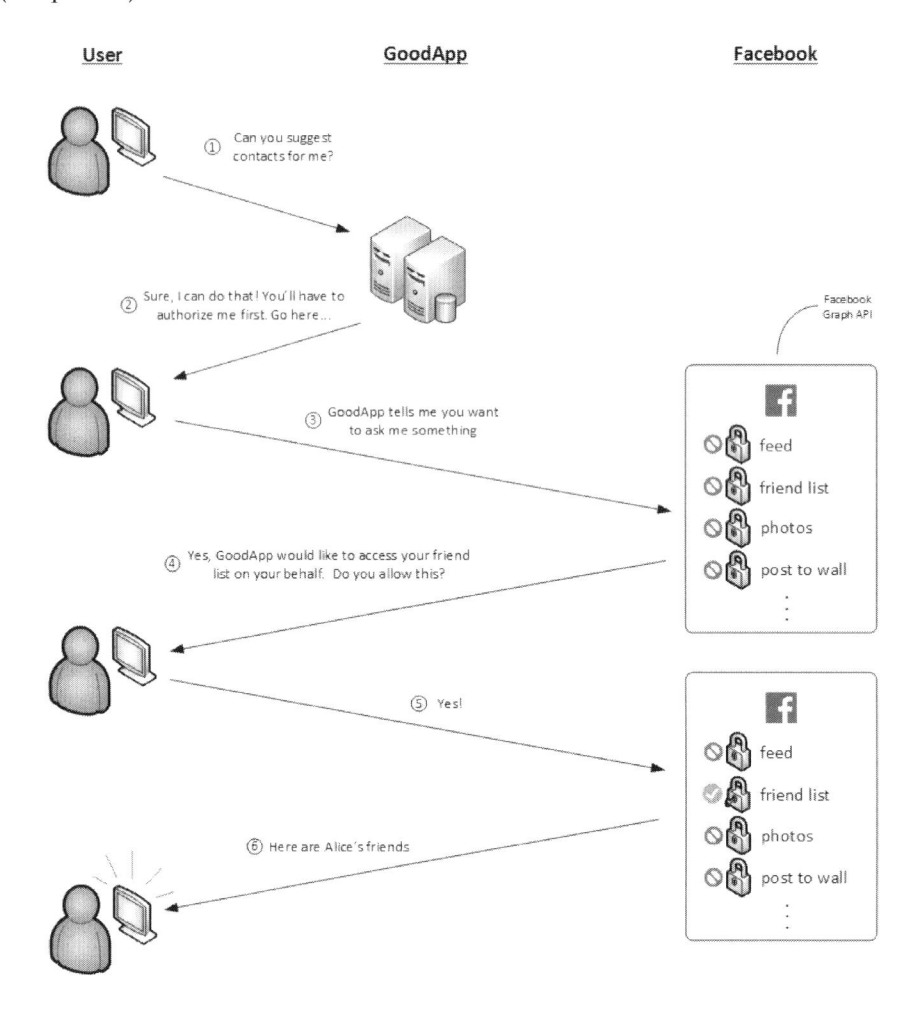

Here are the steps:

1. You ask GoodApp to suggest you contacts.
2. GoodApp says, "Sure! But you'll have to authorize me first. Go here..."
3. GoodApp sends you to Facebook to log in and authorize GoodApp.
4. Facebook asks you directly for authorization to see if GoodApp can access your friend list on your behalf.
5. You say "yes".
6. Facebook happily obliges, giving GoodApp your friend list. GoodApp then uses this information to tailor suggested contacts for you.

The image and preceding workflow presents a rough idea for what this interaction looks like using the OAuth 2.0 model. We will be curating this image and elaborating on particular steps, and sequences of steps, in order to build an increasingly accurate picture of the workflow as it works with OAuth 2.0. The first steps that we will examine more closely are steps 3-5. In these steps, the service provider, Facebook, is asking you, the user, whether or not you allow the client application, GoodApp, to perform a particular action. This is known as **user consent**.

User consent

When a client application wants to perform a particular action relating to you or resources you own, it must first ask you for permission. In this case, the client application, GoodApp, wants to access your friend list on the service provider, Facebook. In order for Facebook to allow this, they must ask you directly.

ized when you want to log into Pinterest using your
You may be familiar with this process already if you've ever tried to access resources on one service from another service. For example, the following is an example of a user consent screen that is presented when you want to log into Pinterest using your Facebook credentials.

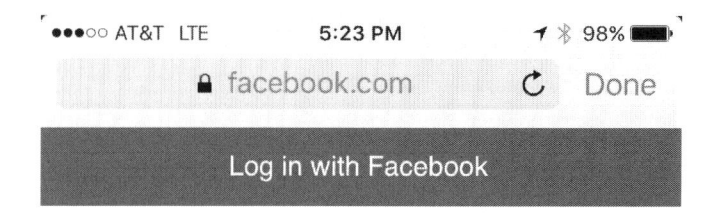

●●●○○ AT&T LTE   5:23 PM   ✈ ✱ 98% ▰

🔒 facebook.com   ↻   Done

Log in with Facebook

🅿

Continue as Charles

Pinterest would like your public profile, friend list, email address, birthday and likes.

✏ Edit the info you provide

🔒 This does not let the app post to Facebook.

Cancel   OK

Incorporating this into our flowchart, we get a new sequence:

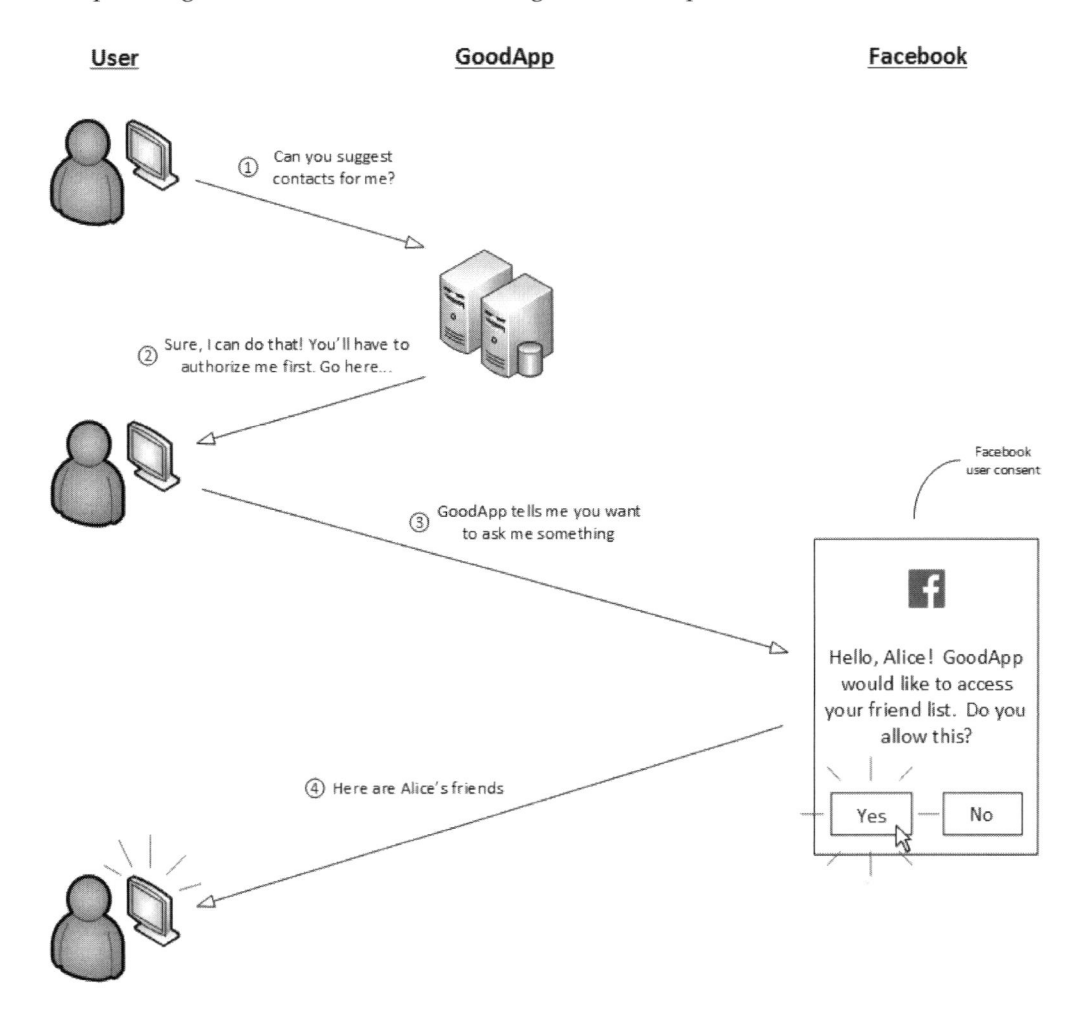

Here are the steps:

1. You ask GoodApp to suggest you contacts.
2. GoodApp says, "Sure! But you'll have to authorize me first. Go here..."
3. GoodApp sends you to Facebook. Here, Facebook asks you directly for authorization for GoodApp to access your friend list on your behalf. It does this by presenting the user consent form, which you can either accept or deny. Let's assume you accept.
4. Facebook happily obliges, giving GoodApp your friend list. GoodApp then uses this information to tailor suggested contacts for you.

Notice how we've substituted the exchange of asking for consent with the process of presenting the user consent form to the user. When you accept this user consent form, you have agreed to allow GoodApp access to your Facebook friend list on your behalf. That is, you have delegated read-only authority for your Facebook friend list to GoodApp.

We can curate this workflow some more. There is a very important step in the preceding process that warrants a larger discussion. It is step 4 where GoodApp and Facebook finally exchange the information that has been requested. In the preceding diagram, we present it as a single step where Facebook gives the information to GoodApp. However, in reality, this is a much more complicated exchange that occurs, which depends on many factors. It is this step, actually, where the bulk of the book focuses since this secure and controlled exchange of information is at the crux of what OAuth 2.0 does. Let's take a closer look.

Two main flows for two main types of client

After you have granted permission for GoodApp to access your friend list on your behalf, an interaction must happen between GoodApp and Facebook to then exchange information. However, this interaction differs depending on the client application and its capabilities.

OAuth 2.0 supports the exchange of information in various ways through the use of different workflows. In OAuth 2.0 terminology, these are called grant types. There are two main grant types that OAuth 2.0 describes that facilitate the majority of OAuth 2.0 use cases. They are:

- Authorization code grant
- Implicit grant

The authorization code grant is often referred to as the server-side workflow, whereas the implicit grant is often referred to as the client-side workflow. To understand the difference between these two workflows and their purposes, we must understand the concept of **trust**.

> **The OAuth 2.0 Authorization Framework**
>
> The OAuth 2.0 specification actually describes two additional grant types: the *resource owner password credentials grant* and the *client credentials grant* as well as the ability to create your own custom grants to suit your needs. However, even with all of this flexibility, the *implicit grant* and *authorization code grant* are the ones most commonly used in practice in the consumer space, and so are the ones we will focus on in this book.
>
> For more information on the other grant types defined by the OAuth 2.0 specification, see *Appendix A, Resource Owner Password Credentials Grant*, and *Appendix B, Client Credentials Grant*.

Trusted versus untrusted clients

When dealing with various OAuth 2.0 providers, there are only two levels of trust: **trusted** and **untrusted**. The categorization of a client into either of these trust levels is determined by two simple capabilities: the ability to securely store and transmit information. These two levels can then be summarized as follows:

- A **trusted client** is an application that is capable of securely storing and transmitting confidential information. Because of this, they can be trusted to store their client credentials, tokens, or any other resources necessary for their application.

  An example of a trusted client may be a typical 3-tier client-server-database application whereby the presence of a backend server often facilitates the secure storage and transmission of any confidential information.

- An **untrusted client** is one which is incapable of securely storing or transmitting confidential information. Because of this, they cannot be trusted to store their client credentials, or any other confidential information.

  An example of an untrusted client is a browser-based application, say, an HTML/JavaScript application, where there is no server available for which to securely store information. All information must be stored in the browser, which is fully accessible to the users and should be considered public.

A Bird's Eye View of OAuth 2.0

> **The OAuth 2.0 Authorization Framework**
> In the OAuth 2.0 specification, the terms **trusted** and **untrusted** are referred to as **confidential** and **public**, respectively.

Notice that in the untrusted example, there was no mention of the ability to securely transmit the information. This is because such a browser-based application is unable to even securely store the information, which already makes it untrusted. Whether or not they are able to securely transmit the information is irrelevant at this point. Clients must be able to support both capabilities, not just one, in order to be considered trusted.

> **What about mobile?**
> Mobile devices are treated the same. Depending on the platform's ability to securely store and transmit information as well as the client developer's implementation, mobile devices can be treated as either trusted or untrusted.
>
> For more information, see *Chapter 10, What About Mobile?*

Now that we know the major distinction between the two types of clients, let's look at the two different workflows that were designed for each: authorization code grant for server-side (trusted) flows, and implicit grant for client-side (untrusted) flows. We'll start with the implicit grant first because it is simpler.

First look at the client-side flow

Let's, once again, go back to our example of GoodApp wanting to suggest contacts to you by looking at your Facebook friends. Imagine that the GoodApp client application is actually a simple web application hosted in the browser. This is an example of an untrusted client due to its inability to securely store information. The implicit grant type is best suited for this type of client application. Let's look at how the exchange of information (step 4 in the workflow image mentioned in the *User consent* section) is achieved using the implicit grant type.

An untrusted client – GoodApp requests access for user's Facebook friends using implicit grant

Since GoodApp, in this case, is an untrusted client, they cannot be trusted to store or relay any confidential information. Specifically, they cannot store any client credentials or tokens. Because of this, they have a very simple workflow. Here is what the exchange looks like, picking up after GoodApp directs you to Facebook for user consent:

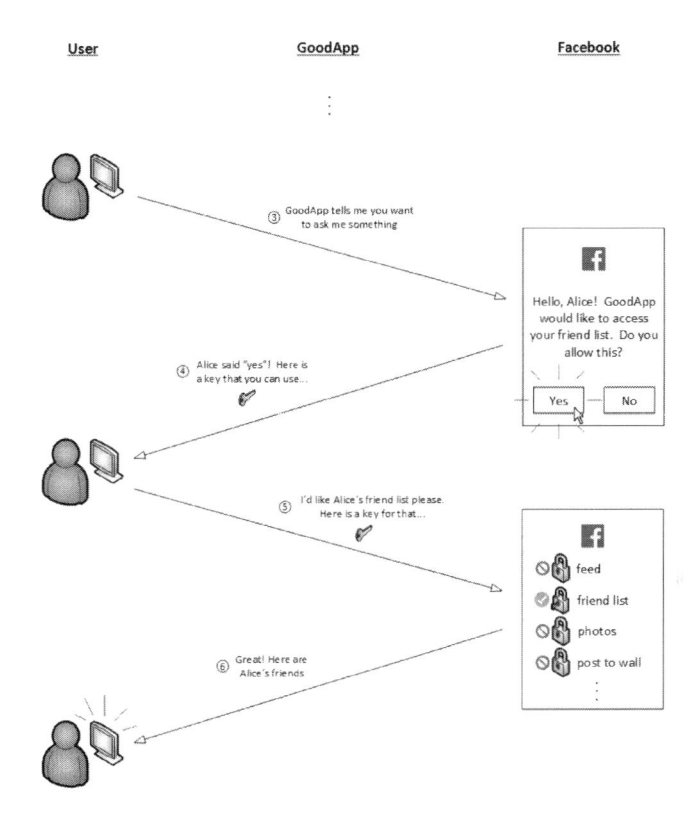

Here are the steps performed in the preceding flow chart, picking up from step 3:

1. ...
2. ...
3. GoodApp sends you to Facebook. Here, Facebook asks you directly for authorization for GoodApp to access your friend list on your behalf. It does this by presenting the user consent form, which you can either accept or deny. Let's assume you accept.

4. Facebook then gives the GoodApp client application (in this case, an HTML/JS web application running in a browser) a key that can be used to access your Facebook friend list. Notice that Facebook doesn't actually give the GoodApp web application the friend list itself.
5. The GoodApp web application then makes a request to Facebook for your friend list, presenting with it the key that it just received.
6. Facebook validates this key, and upon successful validation happily obliges, giving GoodApp your friend list. GoodApp then uses this information to tailor suggested contacts for you.

Once you have authorized GoodApp to access your Facebook friends on your behalf, Facebook sends GoodApp a *key*, which it can use to access your friend list. In OAuth 2.0 terminology, this key is appropriately called an **access token**. This token represents the access that is being granted for GoodApp to access your friend list on your behalf.

Simply, this access token can be thought of as a key. This key only works on certain doors. In this case, this key has the ability to access your friend list, and nothing more. GoodApp cannot access anything else with your account, nor can they access the friend list of any other user with this key.

> **Access token versus bearer token**
>
> An access token is a string value that represents the access you have to a protected resource for a particular amount of time. You may also hear reference to something called a **bearer token**. A bearer token is simply a type of access token. There are other types of access tokens, but bearer is the most commonly used token type.
>
> It is known as a "bearer" token because the bearer of the token holds all that is necessary to use it. No additional information is required. What this translates to is, anyone who has this bearer token, say GoodApp, will be able to use it and Facebook will happily return your friend list, no questions asked. What this also means is that if GoodApp happens to leak this token and it finds itself in the hands of a malicious user, they will also be able to use it to get your friend list.
>
> This is very similar to a physical key: the key always unlocks the lock, no matter who is holding it.

Now that GoodApp has this key, it makes a request to Facebook to access your friend list, presenting with it the key that they just received. Facebook validates the key and returns your friend list to GoodApp, as requested. GoodApp can now craft their contact suggestions for you. Done!

The big picture

Here is the entire interaction between the user, GoodApp, and Facebook, using the implicit grant type, now within context:

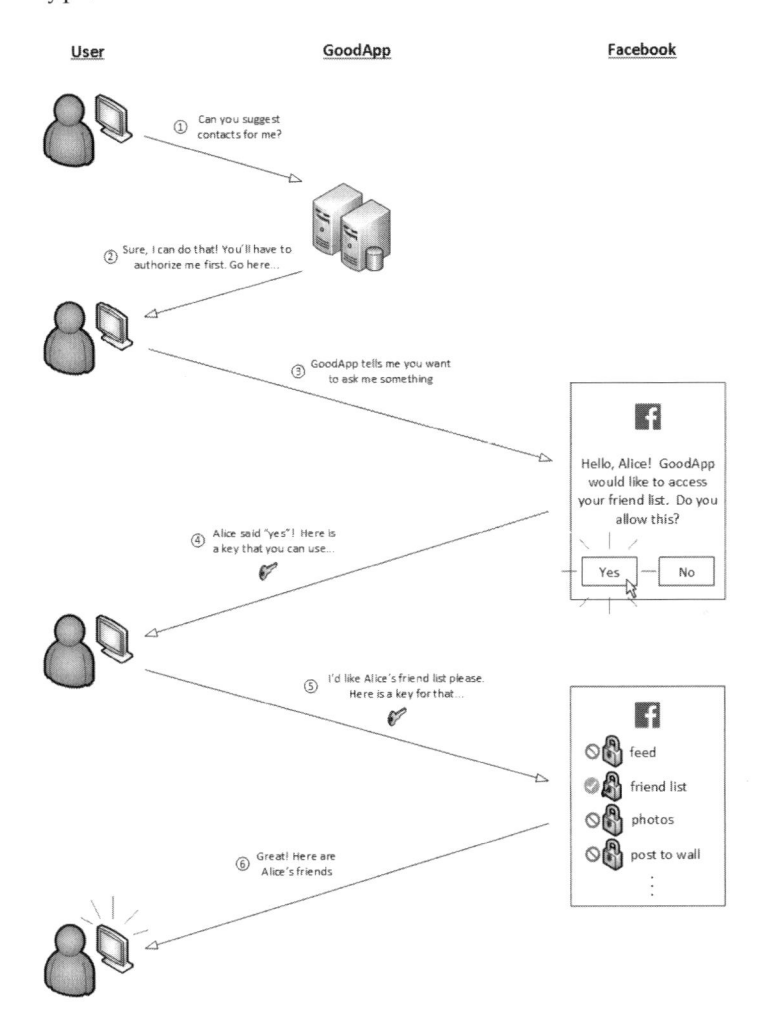

This interaction is repeated every time GoodApp wants, or needs, to access some protected resources on behalf of the user. It can be summarized in full with these steps:

1. You ask GoodApp to suggest you contacts.
2. GoodApp says, "Sure! But you'll have to authorize me first. Go here…"
3. GoodApp sends you to Facebook. Here, Facebook asks you directly for authorization for GoodApp to access your friend list on your behalf. It does this by presenting the user consent form, which you can either accept or deny. Let's assume you accept.
4. Facebook then gives the GoodApp client application (in this case, an HTML/JS web application running in a browser) a key that can be used to access your Facebook friend list. Notice that Facebook doesn't actually give the GoodApp web application the friend list itself.
5. The GoodApp web application then makes a request to Facebook for your friend list, presenting with it the key that it just received.
6. Facebook validates this key, and upon successful validation happily obliges, giving GoodApp your friend list. GoodApp then uses this information to tailor suggested contacts for you.

When should this be used?

The implicit grant type was designed for untrusted clients, and so it should be used accordingly. These clients tend to be pure browser-based applications, such as HTML/JavaScript applications, or Flash applications, which do not require long-term access to the user's data.

Here are some examples of client applications that should use the client-side flow:

- An HTML/JavaScript application running in Safari on an iPhone
- A Flash application running in Chrome on an Android device
- A native iOS application that operates without a backend server
- An HTML/JavaScript application running in Firefox on the desktop

Pros and cons of being an untrusted client

As you can imagine, there are many advantages as well as disadvantages of being an untrusted client.

Pros

There is a convenient pro for being an untrusted client:

- **Simplicity**: Due to the straightforward design, this solution is very simple to implement. Since all of the work happens in the browser, no backend servers or data stores are required for such an application. (If they had these, they could be considered trusted.)

Cons

However, here are the cons:

- **Less security**: The key must be relayed to the browser for the client application to use. The browser is considered public and so this key may easily fall into the hands of another user.
- **Short-term access only**: Since the client is untrusted, they cannot store keys for long-term use. Because of this, the user will have to reauthenticate and regrant access more often than with a trusted client.

> **Best practice**
>
> As an application developer, if you are developing an application on an untrusted client using the implicit grant type, it is best to restrict your requests to read-only permissions. That way, if anyone were to steal the user's key, they would only be able to read the user's data, not modify it. The data may still be confidential, but at least you are minimizing the potential damage that may occur in the case of a leak.

First look at the server-side flow

Imagine now that the GoodApp application is no longer a simple HTML/JavaScript web application, but is now a full 3-tier client-server-database application. This client application is now able to securely store confidential information thanks to the server and database layer, and so is a perfect candidate for the authorization code grant workflow.

A Bird's Eye View of OAuth 2.0

A trusted client – GoodApp requests access for user's Facebook friends using authorization code grant

Remember that a trusted client is able to securely store confidential information, such as client credentials. So, during the registration process (which we will discuss in *Chapter 3, Four Easy Steps*), trusted clients will be issued credentials to store. Here is what that exchange looks like with a registered, trusted client using the authorization code grant flow, once again, picking up after GoodApp directs you to Facebook for user consent:

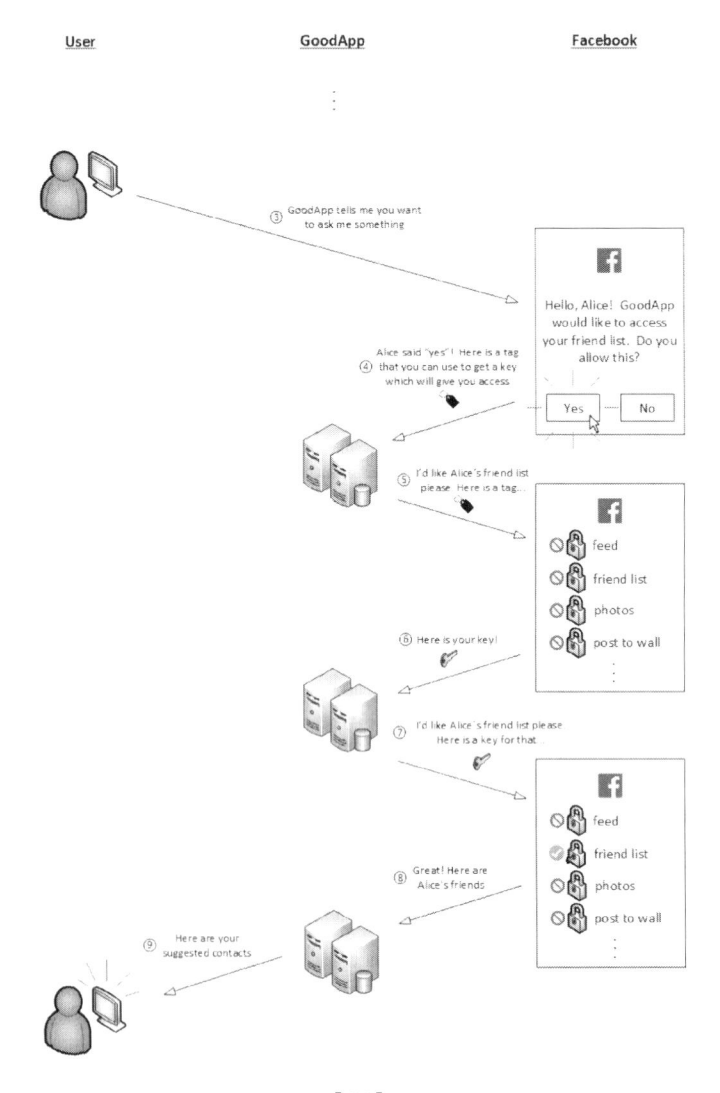

Here are the steps performed in the preceding flow chart, picking up from step 3:

1. ...
2. ...
3. GoodApp sends you to Facebook. Here, Facebook asks you directly for authorization for GoodApp to access your friend list on your behalf. It does this by presenting the user consent form, which you can either accept or deny. Let's assume you accept.
4. Facebook then gives the GoodApp server (not the client web application) a tag that can be exchanged for a key that can access your Facebook friend list. Notice that Facebook this time gives a tag and not a key. Also notice that Facebook issues this to the server of GoodApp, not the client web application.
5. GoodApp makes a request to Facebook to exchange the tag for a valid key to access your Facebook friend list on your behalf.
6. Facebook validates this tag, and upon successful validation happily obliges, giving the GoodApp server the requested key.
7. The GoodApp server then makes another request to Facebook, this time for your friend list, presenting with it the key that it just received.
8. Facebook validates this key, and upon successful validation happily obliges, giving GoodApp your friend list.
9. GoodApp then uses this information to tailor suggested contacts for you.

Once the user authorizes GoodApp to access their Facebook friends on their behalf, Facebook sends GoodApp a *tag*. This tag is then exchanged for a key. This key will have the permission to fetch your friend list.

One important note about this exchange is that the tag used in the preceding workflow can only be exchanged for a key once. After it has been used once, it can no longer be reused to fetch another key. The tag is a one-time-use tag, and so is said to be consumable.

> **A tag is "consumable"?**
> This can be thought of like a coat-check tag, where it can be presented to the coat-check attendant and in exchange, you get your coat. If you present the tag again, they will look and see that your coat has already been claimed, and you get nothing.

In OAuth 2.0 terminology, this tag is known as an **authorization code** and it can be exchanged for an access token, which can subsequently be used to request access to the protected resource. After exchanging this authorization code for a token, the workflow is identical to that of the implicit grant type flow: GoodApp requests the user's friend list from Facebook, presenting with it the key (access token). Facebook validates the key and returns to GoodApp the user's friend list as requested.

The important distinction between this flow and the untrusted flow (that is, implicit grant flow) is that the access token is never sent to the browser! The access token is exchanged directly between Facebook and the GoodApp server, so the access token never gets sent to the GoodApp browser application. Because of this, the access token has significantly less chance of being leaked or intercepted.

The big picture

Here is the entire interaction between the user, GoodApp, and Facebook, now within context:

Chapter 2

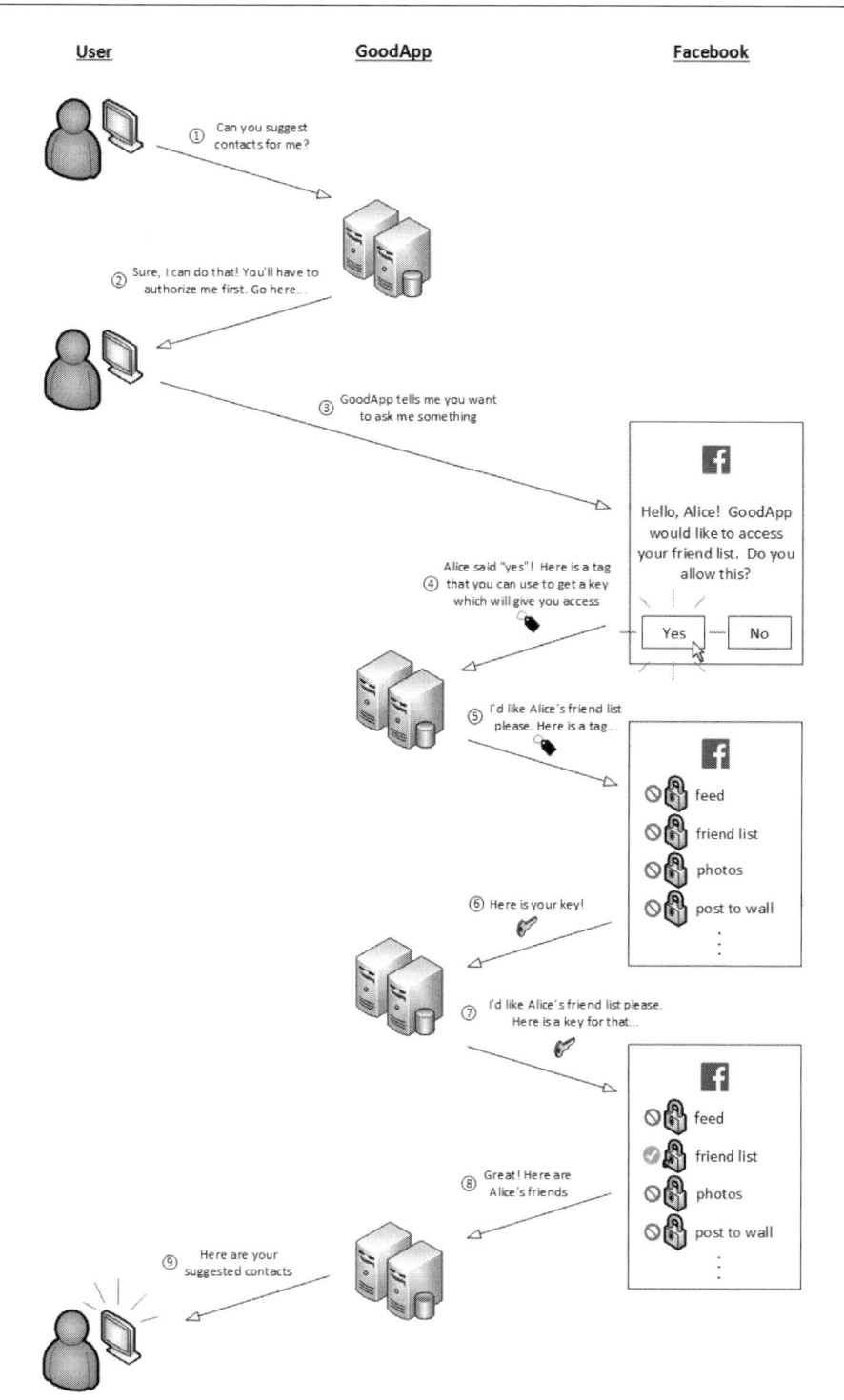

This workflow can be summarized in full with these steps:

1. You ask GoodApp to suggest you contacts.
2. GoodApp says, "Sure! But you'll have to authorize me first. Go here…"
3. GoodApp sends you to Facebook. Here, Facebook asks you directly for authorization for GoodApp to access your friend list on your behalf. It does this by presenting the user consent form, which you can either accept or deny. Let's assume you accept.
4. Facebook then gives the GoodApp server (not the client web application) a tag that can be exchanged for a key that can access your Facebook friend list. Notice that Facebook this time gives a tag and not a key. Also, notice that Facebook issues this to the server of GoodApp, not the client web application.
5. GoodApp makes a request to Facebook to exchange the tag for a valid key to access your Facebook friend list on your behalf.
6. Facebook validates this tag, and upon successful validation happily obliges, giving the GoodApp server the requested key.
7. The GoodApp server then makes another request to Facebook for your friend list, presenting with it the key that it just received.
8. Facebook validates this key, and upon successful validation happily obliges, giving GoodApp your friend list.
9. GoodApp then uses this information to tailor suggested contacts for you.

When should this be used?

The authorization code grant type flow was designed for trusted clients, and so should be used for any client applications that have the ability to securely store and transmit information. These clients are typically client-server-based applications. However, depending on the platform, and the design of the application itself, native mobile applications can also be considered trusted as well.

Here are some examples of client applications that should use the server-side flow:

- Client/server application where the client is an HTML/JavaScript application backed by a .NET backend attached to a SQL Server database
- A native iPhone application that is powered by a server-based backend that it communicates with
- Client/server application where the client is an Android application and the backend is a Java server with a Bigtable persistence layer

Pros and cons of being a trusted client

As you can imagine, there are many advantages as well as disadvantages of being a trusted client. Here are some of the main points (notice the contrast of pros and cons as compared to an untrusted client):

Pros

There are two main advantages of being a trusted client:

- **More security**: The key is shared only between the service provider and server-side of the client application. It never gets sent to the browser, and so has much less of a chance of being intercepted.
- **Long-term and offline access**: Because the client is able to securely store information, they can store the keys and properties necessary for long-term, and even offline, access to a user's data.

Cons

Unfortunately, there is a disadvantage associated with this:

- **More complexity**: To achieve the added security features that make this workflow so beneficial, a more complex infrastructure must be in place to facilitate the more complex key exchange that this workflow utilizes

What are the differences?

The main differences between the server-side workflow and the client-side workflow can be summarized in this table:

	Simplicity	Security	Access duration
Server-side flow (authorization code grant flow)	**More complex**: In order to facilitate the secure storage and transmission of confidential data, a backend server and data store must be maintained.	**More secure**: The server-side flow never exposes the key to the browser, and so has a significantly smaller chance of being leaked.	**Long-term:** Because an application using the authorization code grant flow is trusted to store confidential information, it can store properties needed for long-term, even offline, access.

A Bird's Eye View of OAuth 2.0

	Simplicity	Security	Access duration
Client-side flow (implicit grant flow)	**Less complex**: Due to the more relaxed requirements around security for untrusted applications, no backend server or data store is required. Everything can happen from the browser.	**Less secure**: The key is passed directly to the browser and so has a much larger chance for this key to be obtained by unauthorized parties.	**Short-term**: Since applications using the implicit grant flow are considered untrusted, they should only be given short-lived tokens due to the increased likelihood of such tokens being leaked.

What about mobile?

When it comes to which workflow to use for an application on a mobile device, the same considerations are taken into account: can the application securely store and transmit confidential data. This topic gets interesting when we start discussing modern mobile platforms. Most modern mobile platforms provide APIs for secure storage:

- **iOS**: iOS 4+ SDK utilizes Data Protection
- **Android**: Android 6+ SDK v23+ provides the Android Keystore system
- **Windows Mobile**: Windows Phone SDK 8+ provides the DPAPI (Data Protection API)

> This is not an exhaustive list of APIs for secure storage for each platform. Most modern mobile platforms actually provide many different methods for securely storing your data. This is only a sampling.

Used in conjunction with secure transmission protocols, such as SSL or TLS, many application developers consider these satisfactory for the requirements of secure storage and transmission of confidential information, and therefore consider their mobile applications trusted. This thinking, however, is flawed. Certainly, these secure storage APIs are very secure, and are satisfactory for most practical situations. However, for applications that require a higher level of security and scrutiny, they should be considered untrusted. See the *Are mobile applications trusted or untrusted?* section in *Chapter 10, What About Mobile?*, for a more detailed discussion of this topic.

[30]

Summary

In this chapter, we took a deeper look at the inner workings of the OAuth 2.0 protocol in order to see how the concepts of federated identity and delegated authority are achieved. We introduced user consent and gave an example of where you may have already seen such a process. We also discussed the concept of trust and how it relates to client applications and the workflows they use. In particular, we explored the client-side flow for untrusted clients and the server-side flow for trusted clients. This all culminates in the ability to determine the trust level for a client application, and subsequently, the ability to choose an appropriate workflow for the application to enable the exchange of information in as secure a manner as possible.

In the next chapter, we will look at the overall workflow from a developer's perspective. There are really only four simple steps to explore. This will give us a straightforward template that we can use when we start creating our own application, *The World's Most Interesting Infographic Generator*, in *Chapter 4, Register Your Application*.

3
Four Easy Steps

In this chapter, we will look at the entire process of becoming an OAuth 2.0 client. There are four easy steps, each of which we will explore briefly. This will prepare us for the next chapter where we will put this knowledge to use and actually start building our first OAuth 2.0 client, *The World's Most Interesting Infographic Generator*!

Let's get started

Up to this point, we have been talking about what OAuth 2.0 is, how it works, and how it is used around us. Now, we will finally be able to look at the process of becoming, and creating, an OAuth 2.0 client. It's really quite simple. The process of building our first OAuth 2.0 client can be broken down into these four easy steps:

1. Register your client application.
2. Get your access token.
3. Use your access token to access a protected resource.
4. If applicable, refresh your access token.

> The ability to refresh your access token is only available for trusted clients. In order for a client application to refresh its access token, it must be able to securely store what is called a **refresh token**. This capability is only available to trusted clients, and therefore, the ability to refresh access tokens is restricted to trusted clients.
>
> You may be wondering how untrusted clients renew their access. We will explain this in the *Step 4 – Refresh your access token* section later on in this chapter.

Four Easy Steps

This process can be visualized simply with this diagram:

Step 1 — Register your client application

Step 2 — Get your access token

Step 3 — Use your access token

Step 4 — Refresh your access token

In terms of GoodApp, those steps would be:

1. Register the GoodApp application as a client for Facebook.
2. Using either the client-side flow or the server-side flow, get an access token.
3. Use this access token to get the user's friend list.
4. If we used the server-side flow and our access token has expired, use the refresh token to get a new access token.

As you can see, there isn't much to it! Let's start looking at each step a little more closely.

Step 1 – Register your client application

Before you start making requests to an OAuth 2.0 service provider, the service provider must first know who you are. This is what the registration process is for. The registration process does a lot of things, but most importantly, it establishes a trust relationship between your application and the service provider so that, once established, your application can communicate effectively with the service provider. This is a one-time process and must be done at the beginning of your integration. Once you've registered, you won't have to repeat this step for the lifetime of your application (although you may have to revisit the configurations you set up during this step as your needs and settings may change as your application evolves). Here is a brief list of what is accomplished during the registration process and why:

- **You identify your client application**: This can be as simple as a name, and is used to distinguish your application from all of the others.

> **Why is this important?**
> Without identifying your application, the service provider wouldn't know who is making requests, and, therefore, wouldn't know if your application is allowed or not.
>
> If a particular client starts acting inappropriately, the service provider is able to revoke access to that client without impacting the service for anyone else.

  Let's look at an example. Consider signing up for a gym. Before being able to use the facilities, the gym needs to know who you are so that they can determine if you have access or not. Furthermore, if you start misbehaving, the gym can revoke access for just your key card without impacting any other gym members.

- **You give necessary details about your client application**: There are certain properties of your client application that the service provider would need to know in order to communicate effectively. For instance, in *Chapter 2, A Bird's Eye View of OAuth 2.0*, we stated that the capabilities of your application determine the workflow that will be used (authorization code grant versus implicit grant).

> **Why is this important?**
> If the service provider doesn't know how your application is set up, it won't be able to communicate with it.

Let's now look at an example regarding communication. The gym would need to know your contact details and contact preferences. Without this, the gym wouldn't know how to send you information. Or worse yet, would send that information to the wrong people.

Different service providers, different registration process, same OAuth 2.0 protocol

When registering with different OAuth 2.0 service providers, you will notice that each provider has a unique registration process, and often each requires different pieces of information about your client. However, they are all powered by the same OAuth 2.0 protocol. So, while there are definitely service-provider-specific properties that differ with each provider, there is a base set of information that you should be able to walk away with. This messy process can be visualized with the following diagram:

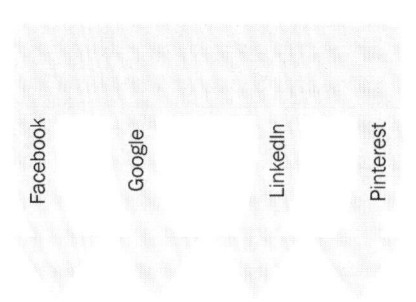

Step 1: Register your client application

- Can register with any OAuth 2.0-compliant service provider
- Should come away with same set of properties

Facebook   Google   LinkedIn   Pinterest

As you can see, the intake for each different service provider varies wildly, depending on the company and how they choose to manage their applications. However, in the end, you should expect a strict set of properties and endpoints that will be necessary for you to start integrating. The set of properties that you should have after registering your application includes the following:

- **Client ID**: This is your client application's unique identifier. Depending on the provider, sometimes this will be generated for you, and other times, you can specify it yourself.

Don't get this confused with your client name, which is just the human-readable name for your application and does not have to be unique. Your client ID must be unique across the entire application space of the service provider.

- **Client secret**: This is your secret key for your application and is used to identify itself when making requests. This will always be issued to you by the service provider.

> **Only for trusted clients**
> If you are using the implicit grant, you may not get a client secret since untrusted clients aren't able to securely store this value.

- **Redirection endpoint**: This is an endpoint that the service provider will use to send you responses (tokens or errors, usually). Most of the time, this will be provided by you. But in certain cases, such as with installed desktop or native mobile applications, this can be determined by the provider.
- **Authorization endpoint**: This is an endpoint that your client application will use to initiate the authorization flow. This will be determined by the service provider.
- **Token endpoint**: This is an endpoint that your client application will use to initiate token flows. This will also be determined by the service provider.

Even though the registration process is different from service provider to service provider, at the end of the process, you should walk away with these five properties.

Here is an example of what those properties may look like for our GoodApp application:

- **Client ID**: `goodapp-541106`
- **Client secret**: `38D83HHFF873RASDPPEKJ1KHJZL`
- **Redirection endpoint**: `https://www.goodapp.com/callback`
- **Authorization endpoint**: `https://api.facebook.com/auth`
- **Token endpoint**: `https://api.facebook.com/token`

With these five pieces of information, we have all that we need to proceed with our integration.

Your client credentials

You will hear references to the term **client credentials** as we proceed with our discussion of OAuth 2.0. Your client credentials are essentially your client ID and client secret. Combined, these are used to identify your application to the service provider. You can think of this as the equivalent of a username and password, but for your application. This is to ensure that the service provider can know who they are delegating authorization to, so that they don't give your friend list to the wrong application.

If your credentials ever get leaked, it is important to change them immediately. Otherwise, this would allow another application (or person) to masquerade as your application, which can potentially have some very devastating results.

> **Best practice**
>
> Just as with your own personal credentials for various accounts and websites, you should rotate your client credentials as well. Set an interval, say, every 6 months, or every major release (depending on the security needs of your application, this may be longer or shorter) where you will request a new client secret and invalidate your old one. This will minimize the impact in the case that your client secret gets leaked.

Step 2 – Get your access token

After you have registered your application, you are ready to fetch an access token. As we determined in *Chapter 2, A Bird's Eye View of OAuth 2.0*, the capabilities of your application affect the workflow that you use in this step. Your application could either be trusted, in which case it would use the authorization code grant flow. Or, it could be untrusted, and it would use the implicit grant flow. You could also use any of the other supported workflows described by the specification. This step would then look like this:

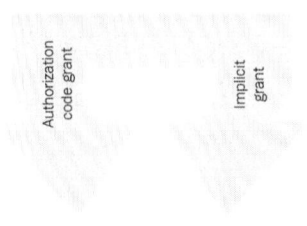

Step 2: Get your access token
 -Can use authorization code
  grant or implicit grant, or any
  other supported flow

Authorization code grant

Implicit grant

The successful completion of a grant flow would result in the acquisition of an access token. This access token can then be used to access a given protected resource. But before we describe how to use an access token, let's first look at what an access token really is.

A closer look at access tokens

Earlier in the book, we made the analogy of access tokens being like physical keys. This is an appropriate analogy in many ways. For instance, keys are meant to protect some resource, say, your house or car, from people or systems that shouldn't access them. Only those holding the key have access.

Access tokens operate in much the same way. They are used by people and systems to access a protected resource that others, otherwise, would be unable to access. However, instead of protecting and accessing some physical resource, such as a house or car, what is being protected and accessed with an access token is a digital resource, for example, your Facebook friend list or the ability to post a status update. The physical key analogy is appropriate in some basic ways, but inappropriate in others. Access tokens are actually much more powerful than basic physical keys. Let's see how.

In more technical terms, an access token is an encapsulation of an authorization to a single protected resource, or set of protected resources, often with a specified duration of access. This is usually represented as an opaque string given to the client. The notions of an access token encapsulating access for a set of protected resources as well as the ability to expire that access are what make access tokens more powerful than traditional physical keys. These two properties of access tokens are known as **scope** and **duration of access** respectively.

Scope

A scope of a token represents the set of protected resources that the token-holder can access. This scope can cover a wide range of protected resources, such as the ability to read and modify any data with a particular user's account, or it can be as fine-grained as the ability to only fetch the first name of a given user. These permissions are requested alongside the request for the access token itself.

In a typical workflow, a user or application would have a need to access a particular protected resource. In GoodApp's case, GoodApp would like to access the given logged-in user's Facebook friend list. So, when GoodApp makes a request for an access token from Facebook, it would specify that the "scope" of access would be for the user's friend list.

Four Easy Steps

If the user allows this (by accepting via the user consent screen), Facebook would issue a particular access token to GoodApp, which is valid only for accessing that particular user's Facebook friend list. If GoodApp would like to access another protected resource, say, the user's profile details, they would need to request a new access token with this new scope.

Further, the client can also stack scopes by requesting multiple scopes in a single request. The resulting token would be different than the first two tokens, and would be able to access all of the protected resources in the original request (provided they were all allowed by the user).

This can be represented visually with the following diagram:

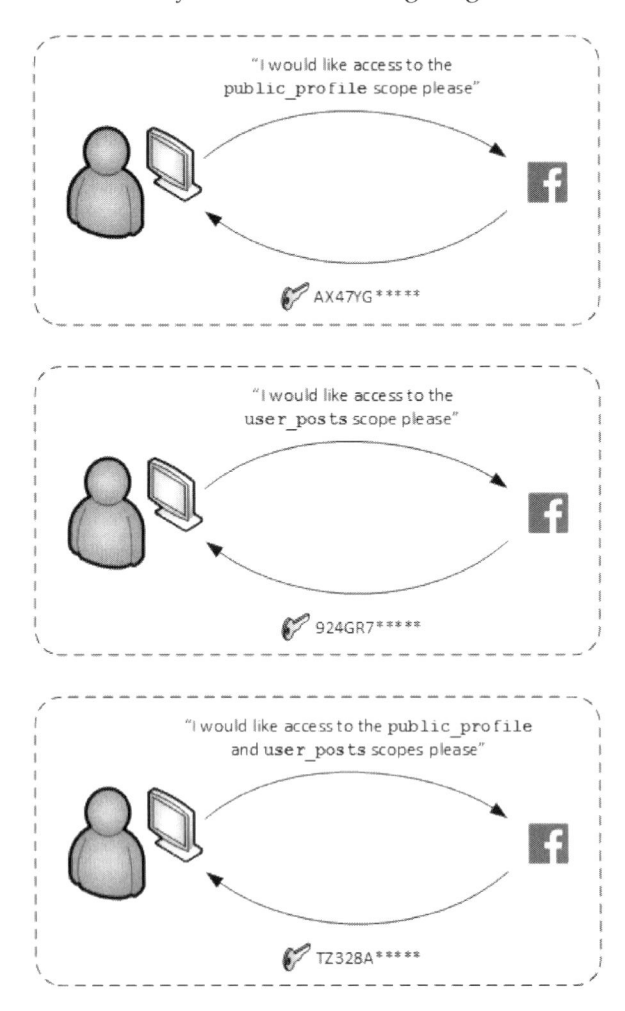

Notice that scopes are requested via some specified string for a specified scope (`public_profile` for profile data and `user_posts` for feed posts). These strings are determined by the service provider. So, the user profile scope string for Facebook may look different than the user profile scope string for LinkedIn. Further, some service providers may not even provide such a scope, and others may require a combination of scopes. For the appropriate scopes to request for your application, refer to the service provider's documentation of their supported scopes.

Duration of access

Most tokens issued by service providers will have an expiry time, a time at which the access associated with the token will no longer be valid. Some tokens, however, will not have an expiry time. These tokens are known as **perpetual tokens** and are quite rare. This is because the repercussions of a leaked perpetual token can be disastrous compared to the leak of a token with an expiry time of, say, 1 hour. Certainly, an equal amount of damage can be done with both tokens. However, the window of opportunity for any potential attackers is significantly reduced with tokens that have reasonable durations of access.

Most service providers issue tokens with durations of access on the order of minutes or hours. A typical duration of access will be anywhere from 30 minutes to several hours, depending on the scope(s) requested as well as the service provider itself. Read-only scopes tend to have longer durations of access than more powerful read/write scopes.

During this duration of access, a token can be used to access the allowed protected resource as needed. However, after this duration of access has lapsed, a new access token must be obtained.

Token revocation

Sometimes, it is necessary to terminate access for a token before its duration of access has lapsed. This is known as **token revocation**. Some service providers support this, and others don't. If the service provider you are dealing with supports it, then you have the ability to revoke access for a particular token if you believe it has been leaked or compromised. This is an important feature, and should be used in any case where you think that your token may have fallen into the wrong hands.

Sometimes a refresh token

If you have successfully completed an authorization code grant flow or implicit grant flow, you should receive an access token. However, if you are using the authorization code grant flow in particular, and the service provider you are integrating with supports the refresh token flow, you can expect to receive in your response what is appropriately called a **refresh token** in addition to your access token. This can be used to refresh a session by requesting a new access token in the case that your current one has expired. This is only returned to trusted clients, however, since this refresh token must be stored and made available for use when the access token expires. Untrusted clients do not have the capability to securely store such a property, and so *refresh tokens are not returned when using the implicit grant flow*.

Step 3 – Use your access token

Once you have your access token, the hard part is done. You are now ready to start making API calls! The APIs themselves will differ depending on the service, but the ways you pass your access token will remain the same. Just as there are various ways to obtain an access token (authorization code grant, implicit grant, and so on), there are multiple ways to pass your access token with an API call. They are via:

- Authorization request header field
- Form-encoded body parameter
- URI query parameter

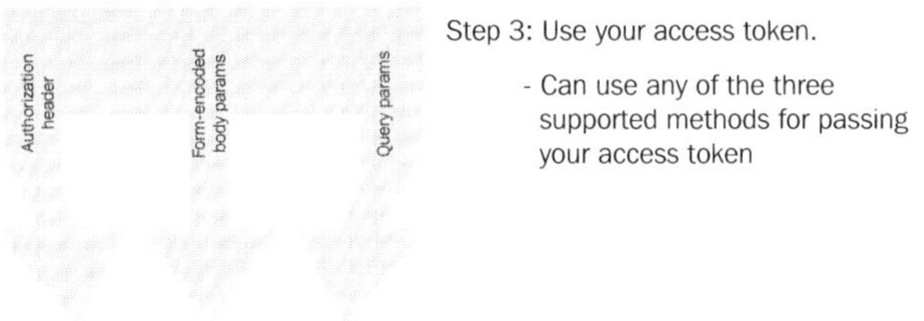

Step 3: Use your access token.
- Can use any of the three supported methods for passing your access token

The details of these different methods aren't important at this point. We will discuss them in more detail in *Chapter 7, Use Your Access Token*, when we actually use these methods to invoke API calls with Facebook for our sample application.

Referring back to our GoodApp example, we now have an access token and are now able to make a request to Facebook for the user's Facebook friends. To do this, we would make a call to the Facebook Graph API to get their list of friends who are also on GoodApp, passing into this call our newly received access token. We can continue to do this as long as our access token is valid, that is, it hasn't expired and hasn't been revoked, and its scope of access allows this.

An access token is an access token

It is important to note that it doesn't matter how we have attained our access token. When it comes to using them, they are all treated the same by our client application and by the service provider. That is, Facebook doesn't care if we received our access token via the implicit grant flow or the authorization grant flow (or any of the other supported flows that we don't discuss in the main body of this book). As long as the access token has not expired and has not been revoked, it can be used to access whatever privileged information or services that was originally granted to it.

Step 4 – Refresh your access token

The access tokens that you receive in *Step 2 - Get your access token* often aren't perpetual. Most tokens issued to you will have an expiry time. This may differ depending on the service provider you are integrating with as well as the properties of your client, but this is usually on the order of minutes or hours. Once it expires, it can no longer be used to access protected resources. To continue to access protected resources, you have two options:

- Start the entire authentication process again. This may require your user to log back in.
- Attempt to refresh the access token using the accompanying refresh token. This can be done without any user interaction, and so should be used whenever possible.

What if I don't have a refresh token?

As mentioned in the *Sometimes a refresh token* section earlier, refresh tokens are only returned in the authorization code grant type flow, and only when the service provider supports it. This is because this flow deals with trusted clients that are capable of securely storing this token value. Implicit grant type clients are untrusted, and so are incapable of storing this refresh token.

So, if you use the implicit grant type flow, you will be unable to refresh your access tokens without reinitiating the auth flow.

Refresh tokens expire too

The refresh token, itself, also has an expiry time. If the refresh token happens to expire and you are unable to refresh your access token, your only option at this point is the same as if you never had a refresh token to begin with: reinitiate the auth flow. There is no way to refresh a refresh token other than by doing this.

Four Easy Steps

Putting it all together

All of these steps together can be represented like this:

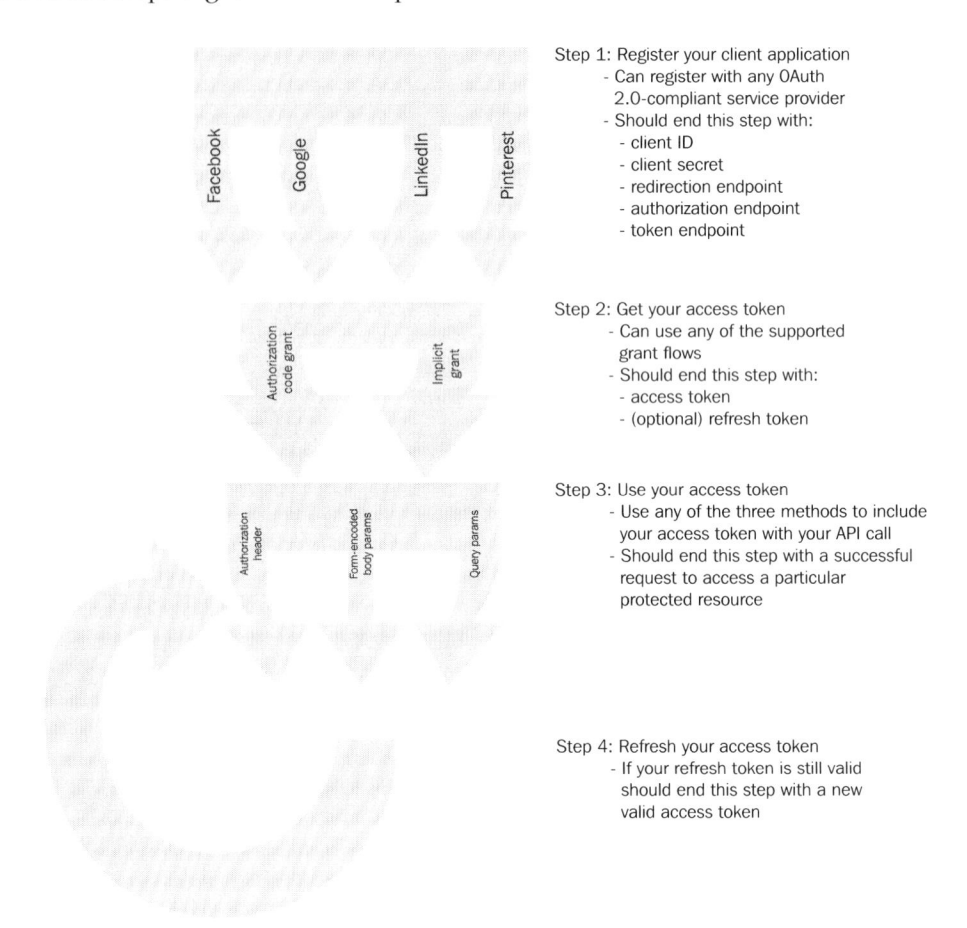

Step 1: Register your client application
- Can register with any OAuth 2.0-compliant service provider
- Should end this step with:
  - client ID
  - client secret
  - redirection endpoint
  - authorization endpoint
  - token endpoint

Step 2: Get your access token
- Can use any of the supported grant flows
- Should end this step with:
  - access token
  - (optional) refresh token

Step 3: Use your access token
- Use any of the three methods to include your access token with your API call
- Should end this step with a successful request to access a particular protected resource

Step 4: Refresh your access token
- If your refresh token is still valid should end this step with a new valid access token

Summary

In this chapter, we looked at the entire process for becoming an OAuth 2.0 client, broken down into four simple steps: registering your client application, getting your access token, using your access token to access a protected resource, and refreshing your access token if required.

We now have all of the information we need to start creating our own OAuth 2.0 client. In the next chapter, we will start building our own application, *The World's Most Interesting Infographic Generator*, where we will start with the registration process!

4
Register Your Application

In the previous three chapters, we introduced the concept of OAuth 2.0, discussed its importance, and even gained a high-level, general understanding of the protocols behind the specification. Now, it's time to start putting our knowledge to use and start building our sample application. We will take a closer look at the process of registering a client application with an OAuth 2.0 service provider by stepping through the registration process with Facebook for our sample application, *The World's Most Interesting Infographic Generator*! Let's begin!

Recap of registration process

You should recall from the previous chapter that client registration is a necessary, and first, step for creating and becoming an OAuth 2.0 client. It identifies your application as well as configures certain properties necessary for the setup and operation of your application. All service providers differ in the way they handle client registration, but as long as they abide by the OAuth 2.0 specification, they will all share a common set of base properties. At the end of the client registration process, the properties that should be known to you are:

- Client ID
- Client secret
- Redirection endpoint
- Authorization endpoint
- Token endpoint

Let's start this process with Facebook, and we will fill in those properties as they become known.

Registering your application with Facebook

In order to register our client application with Facebook, we need to go to the Facebook Developers page. At the time of this writing, this is located at `https://developers.facebook.com/`.

From here, you can create your Facebook application and configure its settings.

Creating your application

Let's start by creating our application. The application creation page looks something like this:

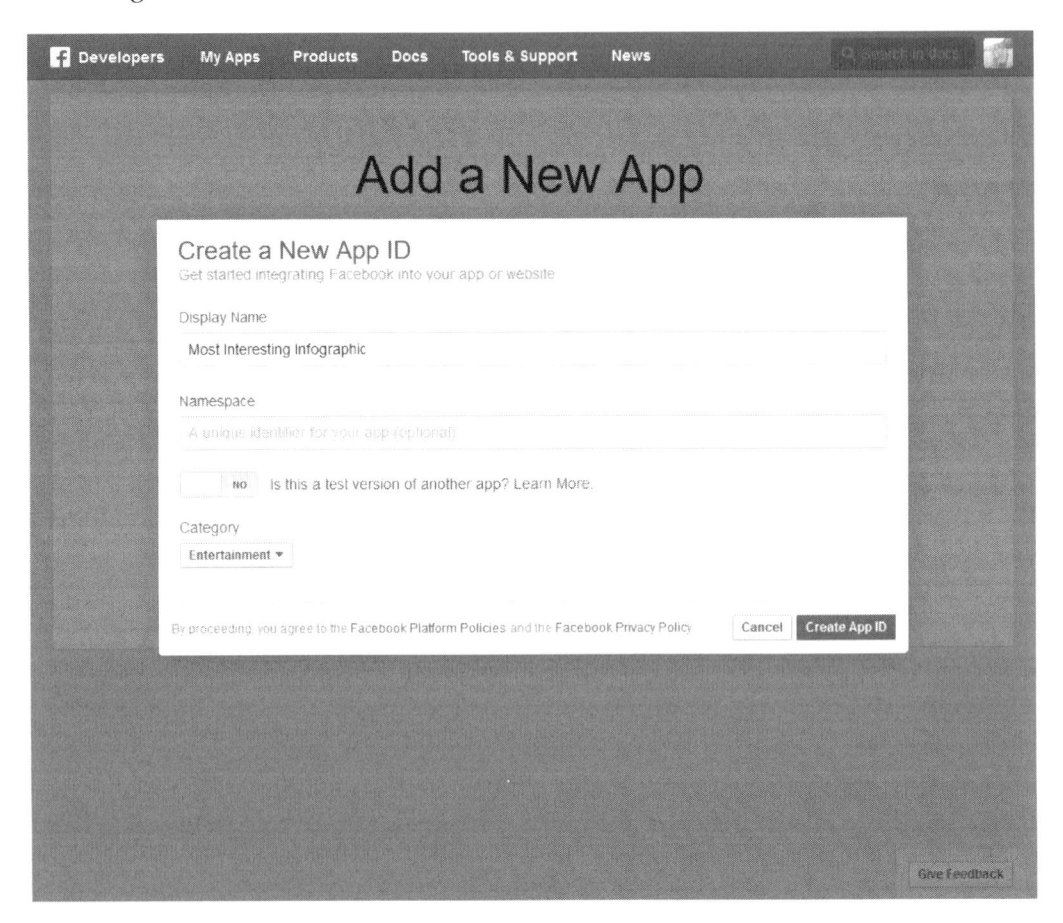

> Display name and namespace are not OAuth 2.0 properties. Rather, these are good examples of Facebook-specific application properties which they likely use for their own application management. Fill in whatever values you wish.

Once you've created your application, you'll be presented with a configuration screen that looks something like this:

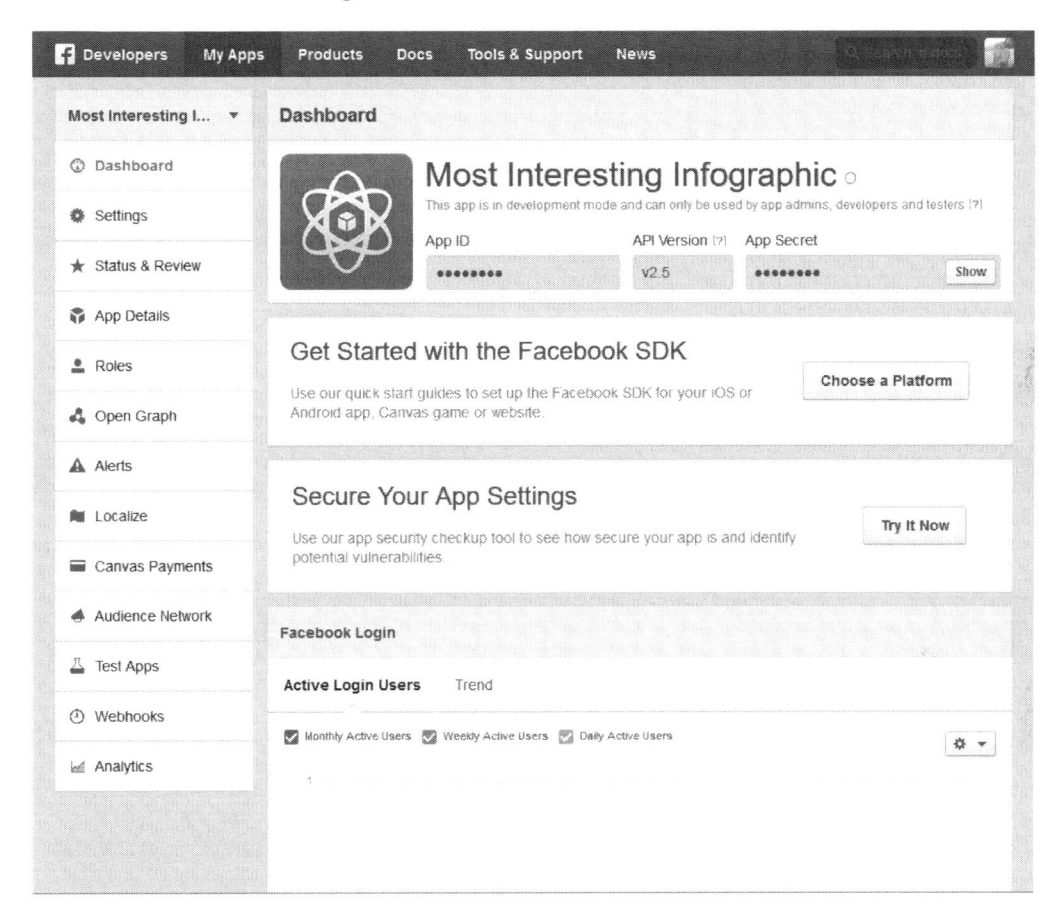

Notice that at the top of the page near the application name, we are given an **App ID** and **App Secret**. This is our client ID and client secret, respectively.

> **In the real world**
>
> Different service providers will use different terminology when it comes to their own particular application creation and development process. Often, this includes different terminology for OAuth 2.0 properties. In this particular example, Facebook calls the OAuth 2.0 client ID and client secret the **App ID** and **App Secret** respectively. Google, alternatively, refers to those properties using the more standard terms, client ID and client secret. Be prepared for this when integrating with your respective service provider.

Most service providers will provide an interface similar to this where you will be able to configure the settings of your application. You can revisit this page at any time to alter your settings, even after your application has been launched, so don't worry if you feel like you have filled in incorrect information during the registration step since you can change those properties at any time afterwards.

Setting your redirection endpoint

Now that our application is created, it's time to start refining our configurations. For our particular application, *The World's Most Interesting Infographic Generator*, the default settings are mostly correct for us. One configuration that we should alter first, though, is our redirection endpoint. Before we do this, let's understand more with what this property is about.

What is a redirection endpoint?

The redirection endpoint is a very important property of your application. It can be thought of as a callback to your application: a way for the service provider to pass control back to your application and even send you important information (such as tokens or error messages). When you start the authorization process with OAuth 2.0, you direct your users to the service provider's authorization endpoint to log in and authorize your application (that is, user consent). Once your users complete this process, control must then be handed back to your application. This is done via the redirection endpoint. After your users log in and authorize (or deny) authorization for your application, Facebook will then send those users back to the redirection endpoint along with any session information (or error messages, if appropriate). It is then your responsibility as the application developer to create an endpoint to receive this information and parse the response appropriately.

Referring to our workflow diagrams from *Chapter 2, A Bird's Eye View of OAuth 2.0*, we can identify the use of the redirection endpoint as step 4 in both the trusted and untrusted flow examples.

Chapter 4

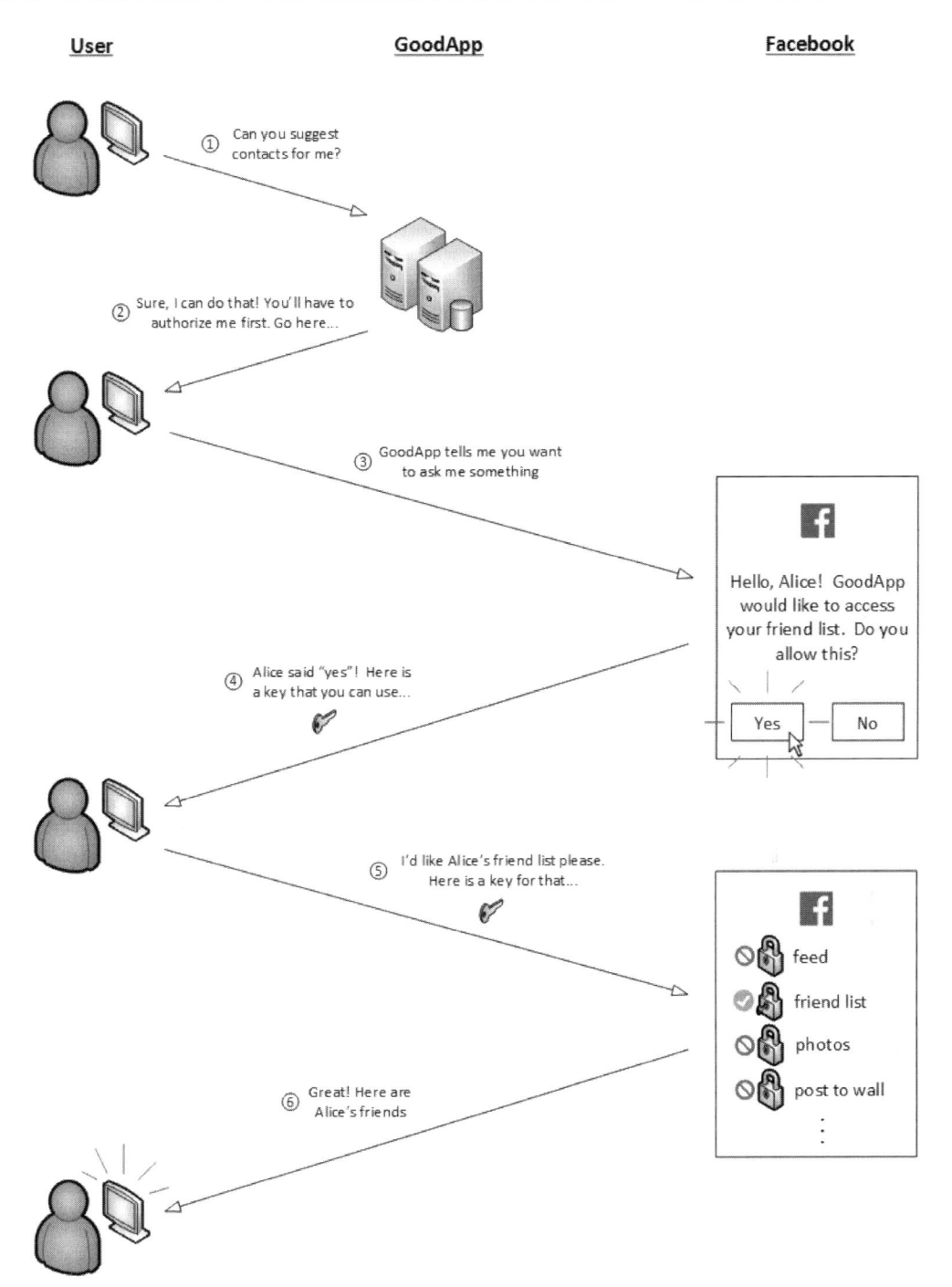

The "key" (that is, access token) is passed back via the redirection endpoint in step 4

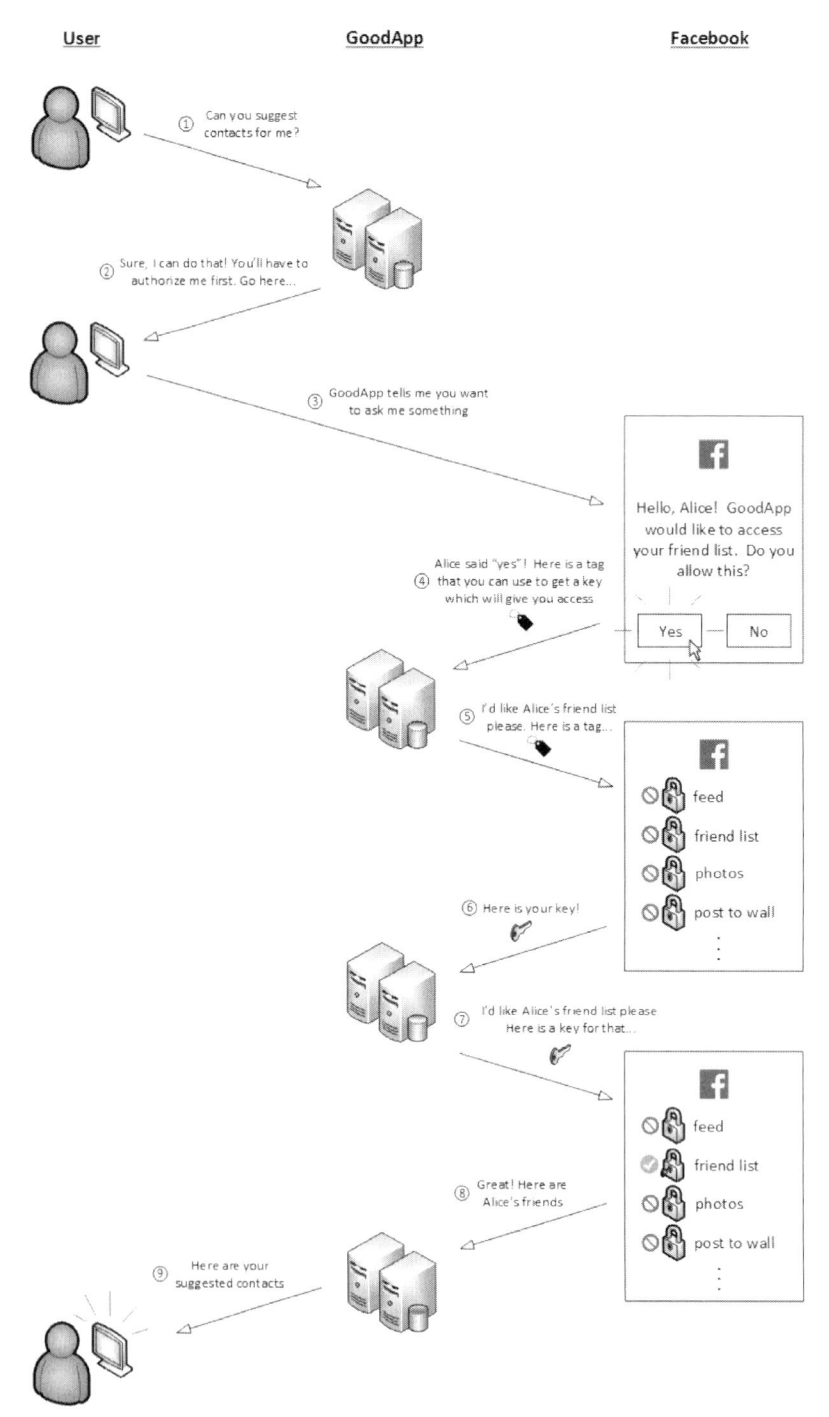

Register Your Application

The "tag" (that is, authorization code) is passed back via the redirection endpoint in step 4

> **What about mobile?**
>
> For native mobile and desktop applications, the redirection endpoint may be handled slightly differently. In the case of a web application, like the one we are creating in this book, it makes sense to create an endpoint on our service to handle this. However, in the context of native mobile and desktop applications, the concept of an "endpoint" isn't as relevant. For this reason, some service providers have different rules for the setting of redirection endpoints for native applications. Some service providers may even provide a particular redirection endpoint to use that your application must detect.
>
> For instance, at the time of this writing, the redirection "endpoint" for native applications with Google must be one of `urn:ietf:wg:oauth:2.0:oob` or `urn:ietf:wg:oauth:2.0:oob:auto` or a localhost endpoint.
>
> What is important is that you can recognize the redirection endpoint from your application and be able to extract the necessary values from the response. This will become clearer when we discuss the process of getting an access token in the next two chapters.

In many cases, when beginning your application development, you may not know yet what your redirection endpoint will be. This is okay because you can always revisit your application configuration settings and enter it when you know what it will be. However, for *The World's Most Interesting Infographic Generator*, we can make that decision now. We will create two redirection endpoints, one for our first iteration of our sample application, and another for our second iteration. Those endpoints will be `/callback.html` and `/callback` respectively.

Register Your Application

To configure this for our application with Facebook, it can be done through the advanced configuration properties page. On the application page, hit the **Settings** menu and select the **Advanced** tab and you can find it in the **Client OAuth Settings** section (the interface for managing your applications on Facebook may have changed by the time you are reading this, but this configuration is sure to exist).

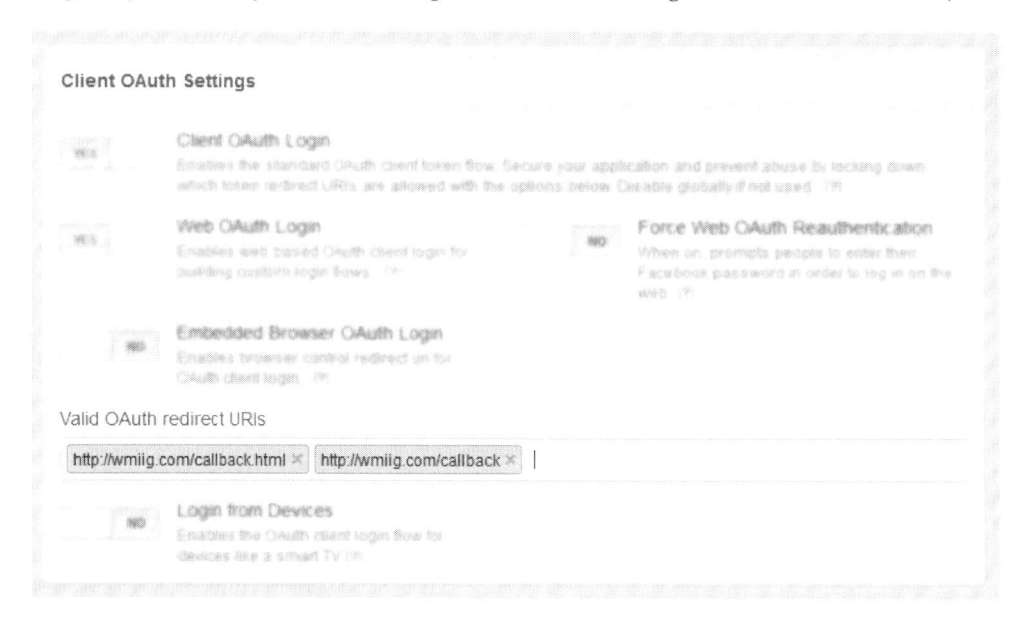

Notice that we actually provided two redirection endpoints for our application:

- `http://wmiig.com/callback.html`
- `http://wmiig.com/callback`

Some service providers will allow you to add multiple redirection endpoints, as we do for our application above with Facebook, and others will only allow you to specify one. Some service providers may even allow you to specify a regular expression or wildcard expression to define the whitelist of redirection endpoints supported by your application. If the service provider you are integrating with allows this, you should be careful with its usage as it can potentially open up some dangerous security holes (see the *Redirection URI manipulation* section in *Chapter 9, Security Considerations*).

Find your service provider's authorization and token endpoints

At this point, we have our client ID, client secret, and most recently, just set our redirection endpoints. All that's left is to find our service provider's authorization and token endpoints. These are determined by the service provider and can often be found in their developer documentation. Some service providers, however, encourage the use of libraries and SDKs to interact with their OAuth 2.0 service, and so may hide these properties. Regardless, these endpoints *must* exist and will be used to complete your authentication flow.

In the case of Facebook, at the time of this writing, their authorization and token endpoints are:

- `https://www.facebook.com/dialog/oauth`
- `https://graph.facebook.com/oauth/access_token`

Putting it all together!

Looking back at our list of necessary properties, we're able to fill in all the required fields:

- **Client ID**: `wmiig-550106`
- **Client secret**: `DFIAJAO98SH9832HVMQI3`
- **Redirection endpoints**: `http://wmiig.com/callback.html`, `http://wmiig.com/callback`
- **Authorization endpoint**: `https://www.facebook.com/dialog/oauth`
- **Token endpoint**: `https://graph.facebook.com/oauth/access_token`

> We provide fake client credentials in the preceding list for obvious reasons. However, you will get your own values when you register, which you can plug into your own application.

We now have all of the information we need to move forward with our integration. Let's start building our application!

Summary

The registration process is the first step in creating your application. The process will vary from provider to provider, as well as the terminology, but the underlying properties and workflows are all the same. Upon completion of registration of your application, make sure that you have the following five properties: client ID, client secret, redirection endpoint, authorization endpoint, and token endpoint.

For our sample application, we were able to obtain each of these properties during the registration process with Facebook. In the next few chapters, we will start building our sample application, making use of all of these properties in the process. Let's begin!

5
Get an Access Token with the Client-Side Flow

In the previous chapter, we stepped through the registration process with our client application. Now that our application is registered, we're ready to start talking to Facebook! In this chapter, we will do this by creating a very simple HTML/JavaScript application, which we will use to request an access token from Facebook using the client-side flow (that is, the implicit grant flow). This is the simpler of the two workflows, and so understanding this will prepare us for the next chapter where we will build a more complex Java application which uses the server-side flow (that is, the authorization code grant flow) to request an access token.

Refresher on the implicit grant flow

As you should recall from *Chapter 2, A Bird's Eye View of OAuth 2.0*, the implicit grant flow is the OAuth 2.0 flow used for untrusted clients. These are typically HTML/JavaScript web applications that do not have the ability to securely store and transmit information, say, from a backend server. Because of this, they have a simpler workflow than other applications using the alternative authorization code grant flow.

Get an Access Token with the Client-Side Flow

Once again, the implicit grant flow looks like this:

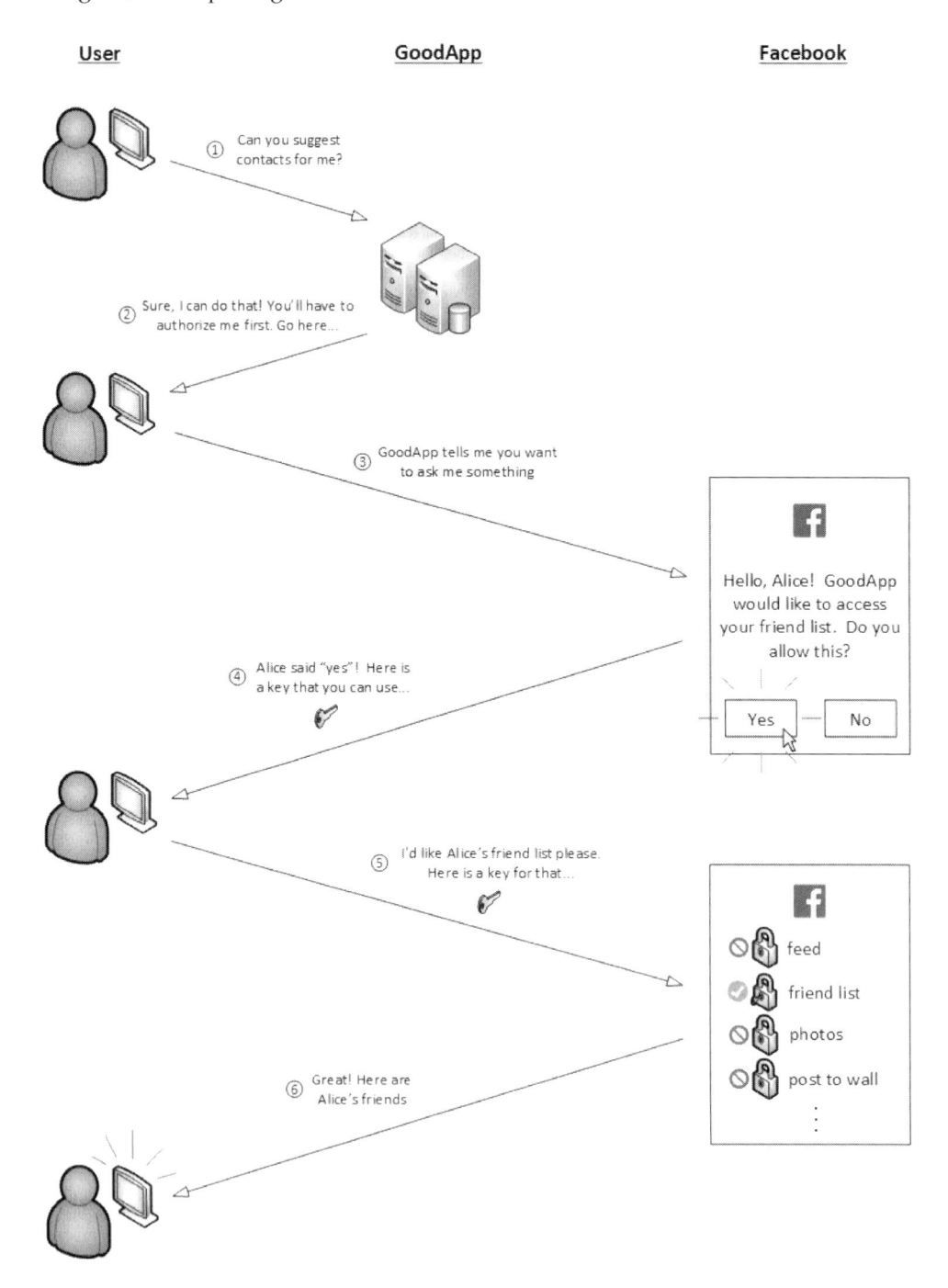

In the context of our application, **WMIIG (World's Most Interesting Infographic Generator)**, the sequence of steps are as follows:

1. The user visits WMIIG and initiates the process to see the world's most interesting infographic.
2. WMIIG says, "Sure! But I'll need to access your profile and feed data to do so, and for this, I'll need your authorization. Go here…"
3. WMIIG sends you to Facebook. Here, Facebook asks you directly for authorization for WMIIG to access your profile and feed data on your behalf. It does this by presenting the user consent form, which you can either accept or deny. Let's assume you accept.
4. Facebook then gives the WMIIG client application (in this case, the HTML/JavaScript application we are going to build) an access token that can be used to access your Facebook profile and feed data.
5. WMIIG then makes a series of requests to Facebook asking for your profile and feed data, presenting with it the access token that it just received.
6. Facebook validates this token, and upon successful validation happily obliges, giving WMIIG your profile and feed data. WMIIG then uses this information to generate the world's most interesting infographic!

This is only a high-level look at the process, just to get an understanding of what is involved. Now that we have a rough idea of what our interaction with Facebook looks like, let's dive in and take a deeper look and examine exactly what is required for our requests and what we can expect in the responses.

A closer look at the implicit grant flow

Our application wants to view the profile and feed data of the user who is using the application. In order to do this, WMIIG must first get authorization from the user. The OAuth 2.0 specification outlines a very rigid, but straightforward, way in which this transaction must occur. In short, WMIIG must send the user to the service provider's authorization endpoint, passing along with it various properties describing the request, including the redirection endpoint and desired scopes. Here, the user is presented with the option of accepting or denying the request. As mentioned in *Chapter 2, A Bird's Eye View of OAuth 2.0*, this is known as user consent and is represented by steps 1 to 3 in the previous workflow. Once the user either accepts or denies, the response is sent back to WMIIG via the redirection endpoint. If the user accepts, the response will contain an access token. Otherwise, an appropriate error message will be returned instead. This is represented by step 4 in the previous workflow. Let's examine these steps in more detail. We'll leave steps 5 and 6 for later (see *Chapter 7, Use Your Access Token* if you'd like to read ahead).

Authorization request

This is the initial request to gain consent from the user. It is accomplished by sending the user to the service provider's authorization endpoint, specifying with it the details of the request. Let's look closer at this step by first examining what the specification says, and then looking at what it takes to make it happen in our application.

According to the specification

The authorization request endpoint is simply the service provider's authorization endpoint with a set of parameters added to the query component of the URL. The parameters must be encoded using the application/x-www-form-urlencoded format. In general terms, the template for a valid authorization request URL is:

```
GET /authorize?
    response_type=token&
    client_id=[CLIENT_ID]&
    redirect_uri=[REDIRECT_URI]&
    scope=[SCOPE]&
    state=[STATE] HTTP/1.1
Host: server.example.com
```

The parameters that can be added to the preceding request URL are defined as:

- response_type: (Required) This must be set to token to signify that we are utilizing the implicit grant flow.
- client_id: (Required) This is your application's unique client ID.
- redirect_uri: (Optional) The redirection endpoint used by the service provider to return the response, whether that is an access token in the case of a successful request, or an error message in the case of a failed request.
- scope: (Optional) This defines the scope of permissions that we are requesting on behalf of the user.
- state: (Recommended) This parameter is optional, but recommended. It is an opaque value that can be sent by the client, and received in the response, to maintain state between the request and callback. It is recommended for use in protection against cross-site request forgery (CSRF) attacks. See the *Use the state param to combat CSRF* section in *Chapter 9, Security Considerations*, for a more detailed description of the recommended use of the state parameter.

> **Reference pages**
> The OAuth 2.0 specification provides a very detailed and precise description of what is required to make a well-formed authorization request. See the end of the chapter to see a set of reference pages adapted from the relevant specifications for your convenience.

In our application

Thanks to the work we did in the previous chapter, where we registered our application with Facebook, we have all that we need to make this request. We will be plugging in the following values as URL-encoded query parameters to our authorization request, which we will be sending to our service provider's authorization endpoint, which we discovered to be:

- response_type: token
- client_id: wmiig-550106
- redirect_uri: http://wmiig.com/callback.html
- scope: public_profile, user_posts

> Notice we are specifying both public_profile and user_posts as the set of scopes we are requesting. You might remember from the *Scope* section in *Chapter 3, Four Easy Steps*, that scopes can be stacked to request multiple at a time.

We are purposely omitting the state parameter. We are saving this for a more detailed discussion in *Chapter 9, Security Considerations*.

Using the preceding values, our constructed authorization request URL looks like this:

```
https://www.facebook.com/dialog/oauth?
response_type=token&
client_id=wmiig-550106&
redirect_uri=http%3A%2F%wmiig.com%2Fcallback.html&
scope=public_profile%20user_posts
```

> **Don't forget to URL-encode your request parameters!**
>
> Notice that the scope and redirection endpoint we passed in as our query parameters are URL-encoded. This is required as there are some parameter values that may contain invalid characters when passed as query parameters. If you forget to URL-encode your query parameters, you will likely get an error response.

It is important to notice that this endpoint is hosted by the service provider directly, in this case, Facebook. When the user logs in and authorizes the application, it is done directly with Facebook and not through WMIIG. This way, WMIIG knows nothing about the user's Facebook credentials. WMIIG never even sees them! This is delegated authority in action!

Now that we have this authorization request URL, we can simply send our user to this location to begin the authorization process.

> **See for yourself!**
>
> Since the authorization request is a simple `GET` request, you can see the user consent screen yourself right now. Simply open up your favorite browser and navigate to the authorization request URL that you constructed earlier and you will see what our application will be presenting to users. Make sure you plug in your own value for client ID as it will differ from the example in this book.

Access token response

If you've constructed your authorization request URL correctly, your user will be presented with the user consent screen where they can either accept or deny the authorization request. If they accept, you can expect a success response, which will contain an access token. If they deny, or some other error has occurred, you can expect an error response instead. Let's look at both response structures now.

Success

For now, let's assume that you've constructed the authorization request URL correctly, and the user accepts the requested authorization. In this case, an access token will be returned to our application at the provided redirection endpoint with all of the important information contained in the URL fragment. Given this, the template for a valid authorization response is:

```
HTTP/1.1 302 Found
Location: [REDIRECT_URI]#
    access_token=[ACCESS_TOKEN]&
    token_type=[TOKEN_TYPE]&
    expires_in=[EXPIRES_IN]&
    scope=[SCOPE]&
    state=[STATE]
```

The possible parameters that can be expected in the preceding response are:

- `access_token`: (Required) This is what we're after! The presence of this value in the response is indicative of a successful authorization request. And it is this token value that we will eventually use to access the user's profile and feed data.
- `token_type`: (Required) Defines the type of token returned. This will almost always be `bearer`.
- `expires_in`: (Optional) The lifetime of the token in seconds. For example, if this value is 3600, that means that the access token will expire one hour from the time the response message was generated. It is optional in that the service provider may not always return this value.
- `scope`: (Conditionally required) If the granted scope is identical to what was requested, this value may be omitted. However, if the granted scope is different from the requested scope, it must be present.
- `state`: (Conditionally required) If a `state` parameter was present in the request, then it must be returned in the response.

An example access token response for our application, given the values we sent in the request, will be:

```
http://wmiig.com/callback.html#
    access_token=ey6XeGlAMHBpFi2LQ9JHyT6xwLbMxYRvyZAR&
    token_type=bearer&
    expires_in=3600
```

> **Don't forget to URL-decode your response parameters!**
>
> Just as you URL-encoded your request parameters, the response parameters sent by the service provider to your application will also be URL-encoded. Make sure to decode them in your application before using them.

Get an Access Token with the Client-Side Flow

Given this response, we can extract the following properties. Our access token is of the type `bearer` with a value of `ey6XeGlAMHBpFi2LQ9JHyT6xwLbMxYRvyZAR` and expires in 1 hour (that is, 3600 seconds). Since no `scope` parameter was returned, we can assume that the scope granted is equal to the scope that was requested (that is, `public_profile` and `user_posts`).

> **Why return values in the response fragment instead of as query parameters?**
>
> You may have noticed that the response properties are returned in the URL fragment of the redirect URI. This is in contrast to the request, where we put the required properties in the URL as query parameters. This is because URL fragments are meant for browser interpretation only and not meant to be sent to, or used by, a server. Furthermore, values in URL fragments are not cached, so there is no risk of accidentally having your precious access token cached on some server or intermediary cache somewhere.

This is what a successful access token request looks like from our application's perspective. However, what happens if the request gets rejected? For instance, what happens if the user denies the permissions requested, or the request itself is malformed, or the protected resource no longer exists? Let's take a look at that now.

Error

If the request gets rejected for some reason, an access token will not be returned. Instead, an error response will be returned. The template for an error response is:

```
HTTP/1.1 302 Found
Location: [REDIRECT_URI]#
    error=[ERROR_CODE]&
    error_description=[ERROR_DESCRIPTION]&
    error_uri=[ERROR_URI]&
    state=[STATE]
```

The possible parameters that can be returned in this case are:

- `error`: (Required) This is a single code representing the error that caused the request to fail. The value must be one of the following:
    - `invalid_request`: The request is malformed and could not be processed.

- ○ `unauthorized_client`: The client application isn't authorized to make such a request.
- ○ `access_denied`: The user has denied the request.
- ○ `unsupported_response_type`: An invalid response type was used. You might recall from earlier that for the implicit grant type, this value must be set to `token`.
- ○ `invalid_scope`: The scope passed in is invalid.
- ○ `server_error`: An error happened on the server that prevented a successful response from being generated.
- ○ `temporarily_unavailable`: The authorization server is temporarily unavailable.

- `error_description`: (Optional) A human-readable message describing what caused the error.
- `error_uri`: (Optional) A link to a web document containing more information about the error.
- `state`: (Conditionally required) If a `state` parameter was present in the request, then it must be returned in the response.

An example response for our application, given the values we sent in the request, would be:

```
http://wmiig.com/callback.html#
    error=access_denied&
    error_description=The%20user%20has%20denied
                    %20your%20request
```

Here, we can see that the error is `access_denied` and the description (after URL-decoding) is "The user has denied your request". It is clear from this response what caused the error, and so you can react accordingly within your application.

Let's build it!

We have all the theory now. We know how to make the authorization request, and we know the structure of the two types of responses we can expect (success or error). Let's build it in our sample application!

Build the base application

Since we are using the implicit grant workflow, which is intended for client-side usage, our application requirements are quite simple. We do not require a backend server to facilitate the calls. So, for this version of WMIIG, we will build a simple web application using HTML and JavaScript to make the calls and interpret the responses. We will be using Apache Maven to facilitate the creation and running of our application.

> **What is Apache Maven?**
>
> Maven is a build automation and software management tool for Java projects. It can perform a variety of tasks, including execution of goals to build, test, and package your application. In 2003, it was voted on and accepted as a top-level project for the Apache Software Foundation. Since then, it has been accepted as a standard tool amongst Java developers.
>
> In addition to build automation, Maven handles the non-trivial task of dependency management. Based on the idea of a **project object model** (**POM**), represented as a POM file (pom.xml), Maven can manage a project's creation, build, documentation, testing, and deployment from this central piece of information.
>
> For the purposes of our sample applications, though, we will only be using Maven to create our applications and run them in a web container to view and test them.

Install Apache Maven

For both of the sample applications in this book (the client-side example, which we are building now, and the server-side example we will build in the next chapter), we will be using Apache Maven to create and run the projects. To download Maven, go to the official Apache Maven website: https://maven.apache.org/.

Download the latest version and follow the instructions to install it on your system. By the end of your installation, you should be able to execute the following command in a terminal on your machine and get a similar result:

```
[Mercury:~ charles$ mvn -v
Apache Maven 3.3.3 (7994120775791599e205a5524ec3e0dfe41d4a06; 2015-04-22T04:57:37-07:00)
Maven home: /usr/local/Cellar/maven/3.3.3/libexec
Java version: 1.8.0_66, vendor: Oracle Corporation
Java home: /Library/Java/JavaVirtualMachines/jdk1.8.0_66.jdk/Contents/Home/jre
Default locale: en_US, platform encoding: UTF-8
OS name: "mac os x", version: "10.11.1", arch: "x86_64", family: "mac"
Mercury:~ charles$
```

Maven is now installed on your machine! Now you're ready to start building the base application.

> **No Maven? No problem!**
>
> If you don't know Maven, that's okay. You can simply install it and follow along while focusing on the implementation of the workflow. Or, if you prefer not to work with Maven entirely, you can deploy the HTML and JS files to your own server for testing. Whichever you prefer!

Create the project

Our base application will start with a simple HTML file. This is easy enough for you to create on your own, but let's use Maven so that we can have a container to run and test our application with. You can choose to deploy to your own server for testing if you prefer, though. To create your project, open up a terminal, navigate to the folder where you want your project to live, and execute the following Maven command on your machine:

```
mvn archetype:generate
     -DgroupId=com.wmiig
     -DartifactId=wmiig
     -DarchetypeArtifactId=maven-archetype-webapp
     -DinteractiveMode=false
```

Maven will do a bunch of work, may even download some files and dependencies, and at the end, will create a folder called `wmiig`.

This `wmiig` folder is where all of your project files are located. The directory structure of the files created are:

```
wmiig/
├── src/
│   └── main/
│       ├── resources/
│       └── webapp/
│           └── WEB-INF/
│               ├── web.xml
│               index.jsp
└── pom.xml
```

> **What did we just do?**
>
> Maven has the ability to create various types of projects based on predefined project templates. We've done this with our preceding Maven command by specifying the `archetype:generate` argument. The flag of `archetypeArtifactId=maven-archetype-webapp` specifies the type of template to use when creating the application, in this case, a basic web application. The group ID and artifact ID simply name your project and give it a namespace. Finally, `interactiveMode=false` indicates to Maven that we want to create the project with default settings for everything else. You can omit this final flag to see what other settings can be configured during project creation.

Configure base project to fit our application

Since this application is using the client-side workflow, we won't be using any server-side mechanisms. Because of this, we won't need the JSP file that was created for us. Let's replace it with an HTML file that will serve as a starting point for our application. First, delete `index.jsp`. Then, open up your favorite HTML editor and create a new file, `index.html`, place it where `index.jsp` was, and put the following contents inside:

```html
<!DOCTYPE html>
<html>
  <head>
    <title>The World's Most Interesting Infographic</title>
    <script src="//code.jquery.com/jquery-1.11.3.min.js"></script>
    <script>
      $(document).ready(function() {
        $("#goButton").click(makeRequest);
      });
```

```
        function makeRequest() {
          // TODO: Make authorization request
          alert("Button clicked!");
        }
      </script>
    </head>
    <body>
      <button id="goButton" type="button">Go!</button>
      <div id="results"></div>
    </body>
</html>
```

This will be the starting point for our application. It is a basic index page with a button and some JavaScript logic to detect when the button is pushed.

Modify the hosts file

In order to test our redirections properly, we need to be able to use proper hostnames when referring to our application. `localhost` just won't cut it. To do this, make sure you put the following entry into your `hosts` file:

```
127.0.0.1   wmiig.com
```

With this entry in place, you can now refer to `localhost` using the hostname `wmiig.com`.

> Since `hosts` files are maintained differently on different platforms, the process of modifying your `hosts` file is omitted. Typically, this is located at `/etc/hosts` for Linux/Unix-based systems, including OSX. For Windows 8+ machines, it is located at `C:\Windows\System32\Drivers\etc\hosts`.

Running it for the first time

Now that we have our base application created, let's test it. To see how this looks in a browser, we will use Maven to host our (starter) web application in a basic web server and refer to it with the hostname we just set up. To do this, execute the following command in the same directory of your project:

```
sudo mvn -Dmaven.tomcat.port=80 -Dmaven.tomcat.path=/ tomcat:run
```

> If you are executing this on a Linux- or Unix-based operating system, such as CentOS or Mac OS X, and want to bind to port 80 as we do above, you will need to use the `sudo` command to do so. This is not necessary on Windows.

You should see output similar to this:

```
[charles@localhost ~]$ cd wmiig
[charles@localhost wmiig]$ sudo mvn -Dmaven.tomcat.port=80 -Dmaven.tomcat.path=/ tomcat:run
[INFO] Scanning for projects...
[INFO]
[INFO] ------------------------------------------------------------------------
[INFO] Building wmiig Maven Webapp 1.0-SNAPSHOT
[INFO] ------------------------------------------------------------------------
[INFO]
[INFO] >>> tomcat-maven-plugin:1.1:run (default-cli) @ wmiig >>>
[INFO]
[INFO] --- maven-resources-plugin:2.5:resources (default-resources) @ wmiig ---
[debug] execute contextualize
[WARNING] Using platform encoding (UTF-8 actually) to copy filtered resources, i.e. build is platform dependent!
[INFO] Copying 0 resource
[INFO]
[INFO] --- maven-compiler-plugin:2.3.2:compile (default-compile) @ wmiig ---
[INFO] No sources to compile
[INFO]
[INFO] <<< tomcat-maven-plugin:1.1:run (default-cli) @ wmiig <<<
[INFO]
[INFO] --- tomcat-maven-plugin:1.1:run (default-cli) @ wmiig ---
[INFO] Running war on http://localhost:80/
[INFO] Using existing Tomcat server configuration at /home/charles/wmiig/target/tomcat
Nov 07, 2015 8:35:13 PM org.apache.catalina.startup.Embedded start
INFO: Starting tomcat server
Nov 07, 2015 8:35:13 PM org.apache.catalina.core.StandardEngine start
INFO: Starting Servlet Engine: Apache Tomcat/6.0.29
Nov 07, 2015 8:35:13 PM org.apache.coyote.http11.Http11Protocol init
INFO: Initializing Coyote HTTP/1.1 on http-80
Nov 07, 2015 8:35:13 PM org.apache.coyote.http11.Http11Protocol start
INFO: Starting Coyote HTTP/1.1 on http-80
```

Get an Access Token with the Client-Side Flow

Open up your favorite web browser, navigate to `http://wmiig.com`, and you should see a page that looks like this:

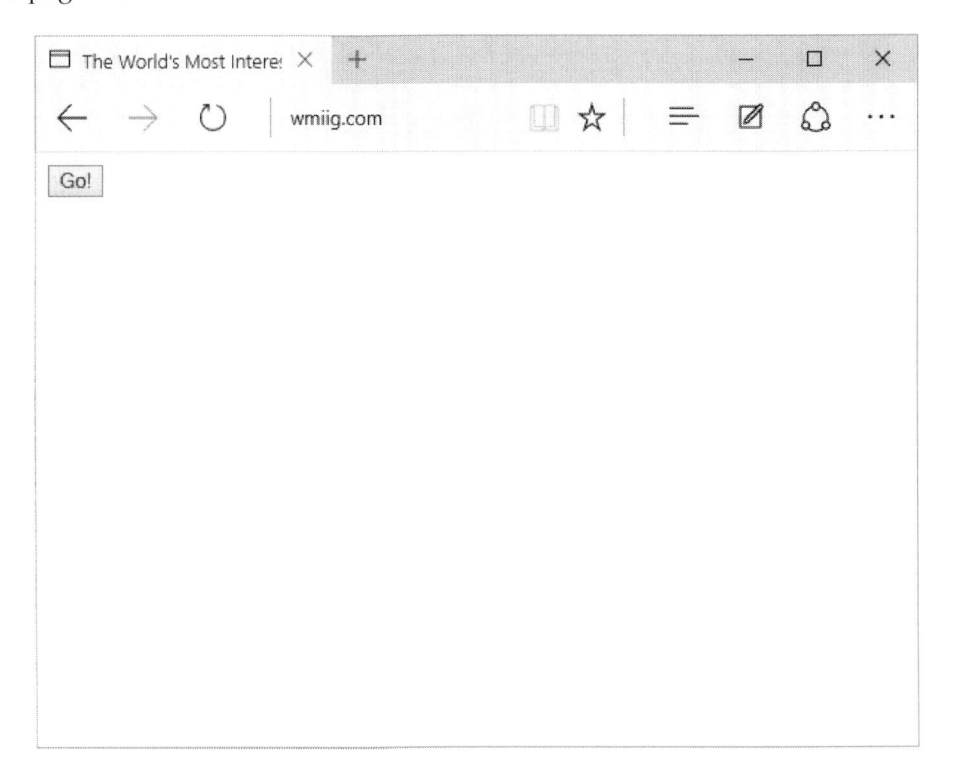

Success! If you click the button, you will see an alert that announces **Button clicked!** As we can see, our base application is a very simple HTML page with some JavaScript to detect our button click. However, right now, when you click on the button, it does nothing else other than to announce that it was clicked. Now, it is time to replace that announcement with the actual request to Facebook.

Make the authorization request

As we established earlier in the chapter, we must send the user-agent to:

```
https://www.facebook.com/dialog/oauth?
    response_type=token&
    client_id=wmiig-550106&
    redirect_uri=http%3A%2F%wmiig.com%2Fcallback.html&
    scope=public_profile%20user_posts
```

Let's do this in our application by replacing our `makeRequest()` function with this:

```
function makeRequest() {
  // Define properties
  var AUTH_ENDPOINT = "https://www.facebook.com/dialog/oauth";
  var RESPONSE_TYPE = "token";
  var CLIENT_ID = "wmiig-550106";
  var REDIRECT_URI = "http://wmiig.com/callback.html";
  var SCOPE = "public_profile user_posts";

  // Build authorization request endpoint
  var requestEndpoint = AUTH_ENDPOINT + "?" +
    "response_type=" + encodeURIComponent(RESPONSE_TYPE) + "&" +
    "client_id=" + encodeURIComponent(CLIENT_ID) + "&" +
    "redirect_uri=" + encodeURIComponent(REDIRECT_URI) + "&" +
    "scope=" + encodeURIComponent(SCOPE);

  // Send to authorization request endpoint
  window.location.href = requestEndpoint;
}
```

> **Scopes are space-delimited!**
>
> Notice here that our `SCOPE` string is `"public_profile user_posts"`. As described by the OAuth 2.0 specification, scopes are to be space-delimited and not comma-delimited like many may assume. Many service providers accommodate both, but it is important to note that the specification requires space-delimited scopes.

Get an Access Token with the Client-Side Flow

With this new logic in our `makeRequest()` method, we are now sending the user to Facebook's user consent page, which we've constructed according to the specification. Save the file, reload your page, and click on **Go!** again. This time, instead of getting the JavaScript alert, you'll be redirected to Facebook where you will be asked to authorize permission for WMIIG to access your public profile and feed data.

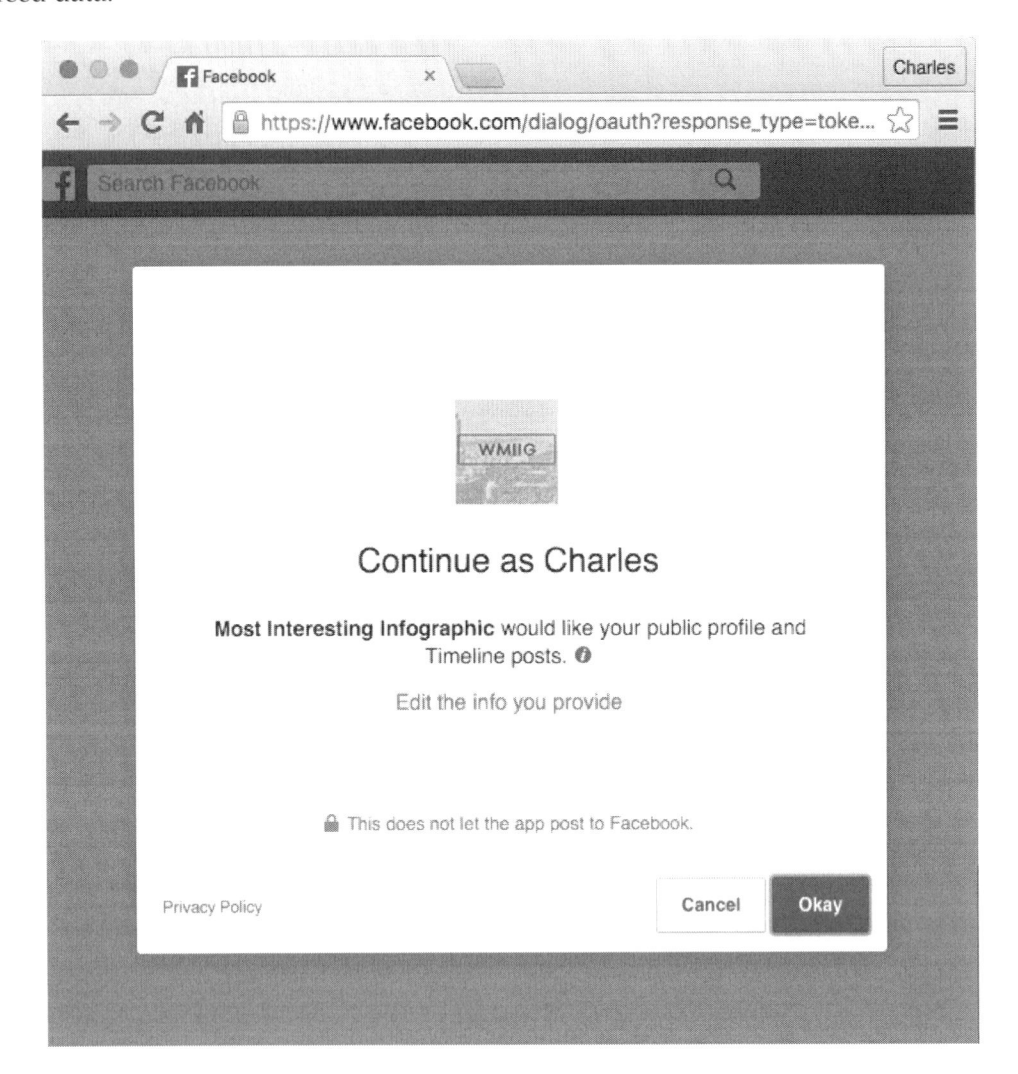

> If you weren't logged into Facebook before hitting the user consent screen, you would have been asked to log in first. If you were logged in, though, you'll notice that you weren't asked to re-log in. This is known as **SSO (Single Sign On)** and is another benefit of using OAuth 2.0. The fewer times you send your credentials across the Internet, the smaller the chance of someone stealing them.

So far so good! If you accept or deny the request, you will see an error page. This is because we specified our redirection endpoint as `http://wmiig.com/callback.html`, but we haven't yet created that page yet. Let's do this now.

Handle the access token response

As we learned earlier, a response will get returned to our application via the URL fragment in the redirect URI that we passed in in our request. We must be prepared to handle this in our application. To do this, let's create another file called `callback.html` and populate it with the following content (recall we whitelisted this as a redirection endpoint for our application in the previous chapter):

```
<!DOCTYPE html>
<html>
  <head>
    <title>The World's Most Interesting Infographic</title>
    <script src="//code.jquery.com/jquery-1.11.3.min.js"></script>
    <script>
      $(document).ready(function() {
        // TODO: Handle access token response
      });
    </script>
  </head>
  <body>
    <div id="response"></div>
  </body>
</html>
```

The first thing we will want to do on our callback page is detect the presence of a response. We can do this by detecting the presence of a non-empty URL fragment:

```
// Extract fragment from URL
var fragment = location.hash.replace('#', '');
```

Get an Access Token with the Client-Side Flow

> **Best practice**
> Some browsers return a hash (`'#'`) in a call to `location.hash`, and others don't. So, it is best practice to preemptively strip it.

Once we have extracted our hash value, we can react accordingly. If the hash is empty (that is, no hash was detected), then we can conclude that no response was passed to our callback (this can happen if people hit our callback URL directly). Otherwise, if our hash is non-empty, we can conclude that a response was indeed passed back to our endpoint for us to interpret. The basic logic for this, in JavaScript, would look like this:

```
// Extract fragment from URL
var fragment = location.hash.replace('#', '');

// Detect presence of response by examining fragment
if (fragment !== "") {
  // Response detected!
} else {
  // No response detected:(
}
```

For the sake of simplicity in interpreting our response, we will simply isolate the access token and write its value to the `response` div in the HTML body:

```
// Extract fragment from URL
var fragment = location.hash.replace('#', '');

// Detect presence of response by examining fragment
if (fragment !== "") {
  var responseProperties = fragment.split("&");
  // Isolate access token and write it to the "response" div
  var accessToken = "";
  for (var i = 0; i < responseProperties.length; i++) {
    if (responseProperties[i].indexOf("access_token=") === 0) {
      accessToken = responseProperties[i].split("=")[1];
      $("#response").html("Access token: " + accessToken);
      break;
    }
```

```
    }

    // TODO: Request profile and feed data with access token
  } else {
    $("#response").html("No response detected.");
  }
```

Adding this back to our HTML code, we get:

```
<!DOCTYPE html>
<html>
  <head>
    <title>The World's Most Interesting Infographic</title>
    <script src="//code.jquery.com/jquery-1.11.3.min.js"></script>
    <script>
      $(document).ready(function() {

        // Extract fragment from URL
        var fragment = location.hash.replace('#', '');

        // Detect presence of response by examining fragment
        if (fragment !== "") {
          var responseProperties = fragment.split("&");
          // Isolate access token and write it to the "response" div
          var accessToken = "";
          for (var i = 0; i < responseProperties.length; i++) {
            if (responseProperties[i].indexOf("access_token=") === 0) {
              accessToken = responseProperties[i].split("=")[1];
              $("#response").html("Access token: " + accessToken);
              break;
            }
          }

          // TODO: Request profile and feed data with access token

        } else {
          $("#response").html("No response detected.");
        }
      });
```

```
      </script>
    </head>
    <body>
      <div id="response"></div>
    </body>
</html>
```

Place this file alongside your `index.html` file. Now, let's start the auth process again. Navigate to `http://wmiig.com` again and click the button. Authorize the application in the user consent screen (if you haven't done so already), and you should now see a page that looks something like this:

Our response object has successfully been parsed! If an error occurred during your request process, you will see so in the response URL where, hopefully, the error code and message are enough for you to debug what failed during your request. Otherwise, if everything is successful, you will see an access token, expiry duration, and token type in the response.

> **In the real world**
> Facebook's current implementation of the OAuth 2.0 protocol does not return the `token_type` property even though it is required by the specification. It is assumed to be of type `bearer`. As you work with more service providers, you will find that differences in implementation, such as this, occur quite often. This happens for a variety of reasons, for example, internal constraints, business requirements, or development restrictions.

That's it! We've successfully requested and received an access token from Facebook which we can now use to access the user's profile and feed data! Before we move on to using this token to request that data, we'll first look at the more complex, but more robust and secure workflow that uses the authorization code grant.

Summary

In this chapter, we took a detailed look at the protocol for the implicit grant flow, noting the required and optional properties in the request as well as the required and optional properties in the response. We put this knowledge to use and implemented a real OAuth 2.0 flow using the implicit grant flow from an untrusted client that we created. After all that, we ended up with a valid Facebook access token. The next step is to then use this access token to make a request to Facebook to actually get the profile and feed data for us to use. We will cover this in *Chapter 7, Use Your Access Token*. But before we do that, we will first take a look at the same process of requesting an access token, but using the slightly more complex, but more secure, authorization code grant flow for server-side applications.

Reference pages

Use these pages as reference documentation when implementing the implicit grant flow in your application. Adapted from *The OAuth 2.0 Authorization Framework* specification [RFC 6749].

Overview of the implicit grant flow

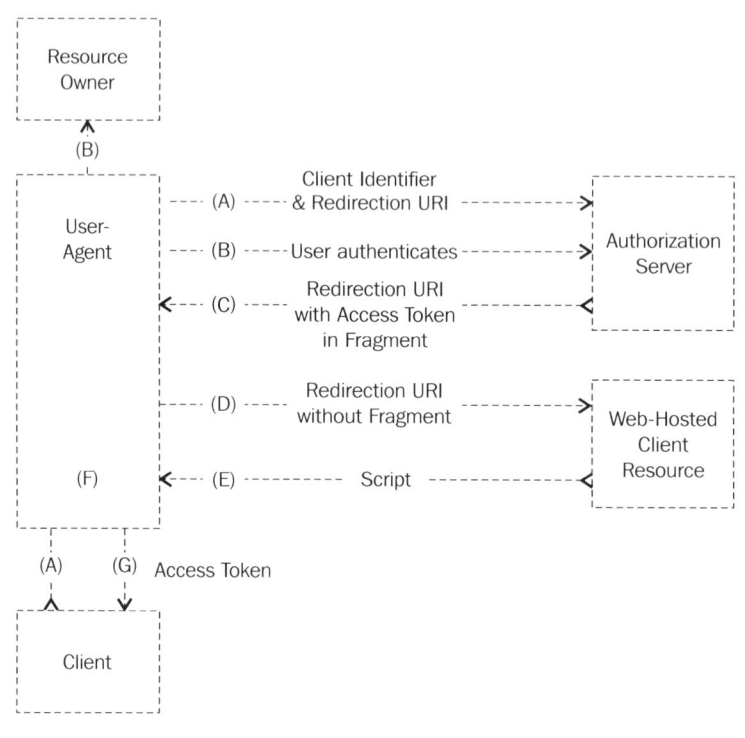

Figure 4 from RFC 6749

The steps are as follows:

- **A**: The client application initiates the flow by sending the user's user-agent to the appropriate authorization endpoint.

- **B**: The authentication server of the service provider authenticates the resource owner and attempts to gain consent by presenting the user consent form.

- **C**: Assuming the user grants consent, the authorization server redirects the user back to the client application via the redirection endpoint provided in the authorization request. The redirection endpoint will include the access token in the URI fragment.

- **D**: The user-agent proceeds with the redirection, stripping the fragment and retaining the properties locally.
- **E**: The client serves a web page that is capable of parsing the fragment and extracting the access token.
- **F**: The user-agent executes a script provided by the web-hosted client resource locally, which extracts the access token.
- **G**: The user-agent returns the access token to the client.

Authorization request

The client constructs the authorization request endpoint by appending the properties below to the query component of the service provider's authorization endpoint. All property values must be encoded using the `application/x-www-form-urlencoded` format as described in Appendix B of the specification:

- `response_type`: (Required) This value must be set to `token`.
- `client_id`: (Required) A unique string representing the client as was provided during client registration.
- `redirect_uri`: (Optional) An absolute URI to be used to pass control back to the client after the service provider has completed interacting with the user.
- `scope`: (Optional) A list of space-delimited, case-sensitive strings which represent the scope of the access request.
- `state`: (Recommended) An opaque value used by the client to maintain state between the request and callback. This parameter should be used for the prevention of cross-site request forgery as described in Section 10.12 of the specification.

An example authorization request looks like this:

```
GET /authorize?
  response_type=token&
  client_id=s6BhdRkqt3&
  state=xyz&
  redirect_uri=https%3A%2F%Eexample%2Ecom%2Fcallback HTTP/1.1
Host: server.example.com
```

Access token response

If the user grants access to the protected resource to the client application, the success response will be sent to the client application in the URL fragment of the redirect URI with the following properties encoded using the `application/x-www-form-urlencoded` format as described in Appendix B of the specification:

- `access_token`: (Required) The access token issued by the service provider.
- `token_type`: (Required) The type of the token issued. This value is case-insensitive.
- `expires_in`: (Optional) The lifetime of the access token given in seconds. If omitted, the service provider should communicate the expiration time via other means.
- `scope`: (Conditionally required) A list of space-delimited, case-sensitive strings which represent the scope of the access granted. Required only if the scope granted is different from the scope requested.
- `state`: (Conditionally required) Required only if the `state` parameter was present in the authorization request. Must be the same value as was received by the client.

An example access token response looks like this:

```
HTTP/1.1 302 Found
Location: http://example.com/callback#
   access_token=2YotnFZFEjr1zCsicMWpAA&
   state=xyz&
   token_type=bearer&
   expires_in=3600
```

Error response

If the access request fails for any reason, the error response will be sent to the client application in the URL fragment of the redirect URI with the following properties encoded using the `application/x-www-form-urlencoded` format as described in Appendix B of the specification:

- `error`: (Required) This is a single error code representing the condition that caused the request to fail. The value must be one of the following:
  - `invalid_request`: The request is missing a required parameter, includes an invalid parameter value, includes a parameter more than once, or is otherwise malformed.

- ○ `unauthorized_client`: The client is not authorized to use this method to request an access token.
- ○ `access_denied`: The user or service provider denied the request.
- ○ `unsupported_response_type`: The service provider does not support obtaining an access token using this method.
- ○ `invalid_scope`: The requested scope is invalid, unknown, or malformed.
- ○ `server_error`: The service provider encountered an unexpected error that prevented it from fulfilling the request. This error code is necessary because an HTTP 500 (Internal Server Error) status code cannot be returned to the client via an HTTP redirect.)
- ○ `temporarily_unavailable`: The authorization server is currently unable to handle the request. This error code is necessary because an HTTP 503 (Service Unavailable) status code cannot be returned to the client via an HTTP redirect.

- `error_description`: (Optional) Human-readable ASCII message providing additional information regarding the error.
- `error_uri`: (Optional) A URI identifying a human-readable web page providing additional information regarding the error.

An example error response looks like this:

```
HTTP/1.1 302 Found
Location: https://example.com/callback#
  error=access_denied&
  state=xyz
```

6
Get an Access Token with the Server-Side Flow

In the previous chapter, we looked at how to obtain an access token using the client-side flow (that is, the implicit grant flow). We demonstrated this by creating a very simple HTML/JavaScript application that requested an access token from Facebook using the credentials we created in *Chapter 4, Register Your Application*.

In this chapter, we will take a closer look at the server-side flow for getting an access token. Just as we did for the client-side flow in the previous chapter, we will look at the request and response structure necessary to make successful calls to an OAuth 2.0 service provider. We will then create a simple Java application, and use our knowledge to request an access token from the server side using the slightly more complex, but more secure, server-side flow (that is, authorization code grant flow).

Refresher on the authorization code grant flow

Recall from *Chapter 2, A Bird's Eye View of OAuth 2.0*, the authorization code grant flow is the OAuth 2.0 flow used for trusted clients. These are typically web applications powered by some sort of backend. For example, an HTML/JS frontend powered by a Python server, or a Flash frontend powered by a Ruby on Rails backend. For our sample application, WMIIG, we will be building an HTML/JS frontend powered by a Java backend.

Get an Access Token with the Server-Side Flow

The addition of a server-side to the access token workflow makes the authorization code grant flow more secure and more powerful than the client-side implicit grant flow. We will see how as we proceed through this chapter. For now, recall that the authorization code grant flow looks like this:

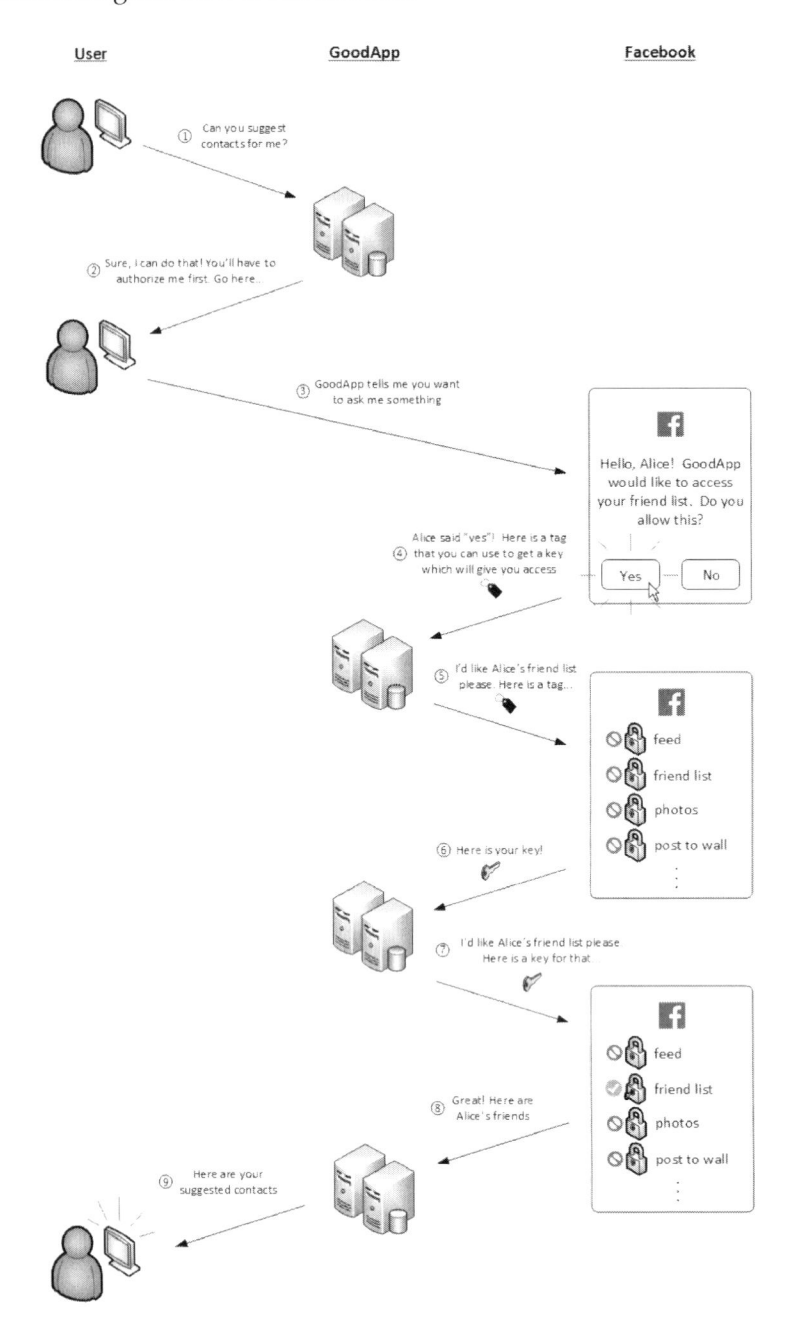

In the context of our application, **WMIIG (World's Most Interesting Infographic Generator)**, the sequence of steps would be as follows:

1. The user visits WMIIG and initiates the process to see the world's most interesting infographic.
2. WMIIG says: "Sure! But I'll need to access your profile and feed data to do so, and for that, I'll need your authorization. Go here…"
3. WMIIG sends you to Facebook. Here, Facebook asks you directly for authorization for WMIIG to access your profile and feed data on your behalf. It does this by presenting the user consent form, which you can either accept or deny. Let's assume you accept.
4. Facebook then gives the WMIIG server (not the HTML/JS application) an authorization code that can be exchanged for an access token that can access your Facebook profile and feed data. Notice that Facebook this time gives an authorization code and not an access token. Also notice that Facebook issues this to the server of WMIIG, not the HTML/JS client application.
5. WMIIG makes a request to Facebook to exchange the authorization code for a valid access token to access your Facebook profile and feed data on your behalf.
6. Facebook validates your authorization code, and upon successful validation happily obliges, giving WMIIG server a valid access token.
7. WMIIG server then makes a series of requests to Facebook asking for your profile and feed data, presenting with it the access token that it just received.
8. Facebook validates this access token, and upon successful validation happily obliges, giving WMIIG your friend list.
9. WMIIG then uses this information to generate the world's most interesting infographic!

> **An important difference**
>
> It is this added step of "exchanging" the authorization code for an access token from the server side that differentiates the authorization code grant flow from the implicit grant flow. In order for the server to do this, it must securely maintain, and securely transmit, its client credentials and tokens. An untrusted client is unable to securely store these credentials (no, the browser is not considered secure), and therefore is unable to use the trusted, authorization code grant flow.

This is a high-level look at the process. With this in mind, we can dive in and take a closer look at the specific requests and responses involved in getting an access token from the service provider using the authorization code grant flow.

A closer look at the authorization code grant flow

Our server-side application would like to view the profile and feed data of the user who is using the application. In order to do this, WMIIG must first get authorization from the user by sending them to the service provider's authorization endpoint, passing along with it various properties describing the request. This step is nearly identical to how we did it for the implicit grant flow, with one important difference which we will get to shortly.

Here, the user is presented with the user consent screen, where they have the option of either accepting or denying the request. Once the user either accepts or denies, the response is sent back to WMIIG via the redirection endpoint. If the user accepts, the response will contain an authorization code, which can then be exchanged for an access token. Otherwise, an appropriate error message will be returned instead. This is represented by steps 4-6 in the preceding workflow. Let's examine these steps in more detail. We'll leave steps 7-9 for the next chapter, *Chapter 7, Use Your Access Token*, where we discuss how to actually use this access token to request access to a protected resource.

Authorization request

The authorization request is the initial request to gain consent from the user. As we mentioned earlier, it is nearly identical to the authorization request we made in the previous chapter for the implicit grant flow, except for one important difference: the value of the `response_type` parameter must be set to `code` instead of `token`. Making this small change will indicate to the service provider that we are invoking the authorization code grant flow instead of the implicit grant flow. Let's take a closer look at this step for the authorization code grant flow.

According to the specification

The authorization request endpoint is simply the service provider's authorization endpoint with a set of parameters added to the query component of the URL. The parameters must be encoded using the `application/x-www-form-urlencoded` format. In general terms, the template for a valid authorization request URL is:

```
GET /authorize?
    response_type=code&
    client_id=[CLIENT_ID]&
    redirect_uri=[REDIRECT_URI]&
    scope=[SCOPE]&
    state=[STATE] HTTP/1.1
Host: server.example.com
```

The parameters that can be added to the preceding request URL are defined as:

- `response_type`: (Required) This must be set to `code` to signify that we are utilizing the authorization code grant flow.
- `client_id`: (Required) This is your application's unique client ID.
- `redirect_uri`: (Optional) The redirection endpoint used by the service provider to return the response, whether that is an access token in the case of a successful request, or an error message in the case of a failed request.
- `scope`: (Optional) This defines the scope of permissions that we are requesting on behalf of the user.
- `state`: (Recommended) This parameter is optional, but recommended. It is an opaque value that can be sent by the client, and received in the response, to maintain the state between the request and callback. It's use is recommended for protecting against cross-site request forgery (CSRF) attacks. See the *Use the state param to combat CSRF* section in *Chapter 9, Security Considerations*, for a more detailed description of the recommended use of the `state` parameter.

> **I think I've seen this before...**
>
> Notice, this initial request to the service provider is nearly identical to the one used in the implicit grant. The only difference is that the `response_type` parameter must be set to `code` rather than `token` to signify that we are indeed using a different workflow.

In our application

Just as we did in the previous chapter, we will be plugging in the values that we obtained in *Chapter 4, Register Your Application*, to our authorization request:

- `response_type`: code
- `client_id`: wmiig 550106
- `redirect_uri`: http://wmiig.com/callback
- `scope`: public_profile, user_posts

Using the preceding values, our constructed authorization request URL looks like this:

```
https://www.facebook.com/dialog/oauth?
    response_type=code&
    client_id=wmiig-550106&
    redirect_uri=http%3A%2F%2Fwmiig.com%2Fcallback&
    scope=public_profile%20user_posts
```

Once here, the user will be asked to identify themselves by logging in (if they haven't already). Once logged in, they are asked to authorize the permissions requested by the application. This is the same user consent screen we described in the last chapter.

> **See for yourself!**
>
> Just as we did in the last chapter to test the authorization request URL, we can do that here too. Navigate to the preceding URL in your favorite browser to see what your users will see. Don't forget to plug in your own value for client ID as it will differ from the example in this book.

Authorization response

If you've constructed your authorization request URL correctly, your user will be presented with the user consent screen, where they can either accept or deny the authorization request. If they accept, you can expect a success response, which will contain an authorization code, which you can then exchange for an access token. This is represented as step 4 in the diagram of the *Refresher on the authorization code grant flow* section. Note, this is different from the implicit grant flow where an access token is returned directly. If the user denies the request, or some other error has occurred, you can expect an error response instead. Let's look at both response structures now.

Success

For now, let's assume that you've constructed the request URL correctly, and the user accepts the requested authorization. In this case, an authorization code will be returned to our application at the provided redirection endpoint with all of the important information contained in the URL query component. Given this, the template for a valid authorization response is:

```
HTTP/1.1 302 Found
Location: [REDIRECT_URI]?
    code=[AUTHORIZATION_CODE]&
    state=[STATE]
```

> **Response values in the query component, not fragment**
>
> It is important to note that the response values are returned in the query component of the redirection endpoint as opposed to the URL fragment, as is done with the implicit code grant flow. Make sure to parse this response accordingly. Otherwise, you will never properly detect the presence of the authorization code (or error code) in the response.

The possible parameters that can be expected in the preceding response are:

- `code`: (Required) This is the value of the authorization code that we use to exchange for an access token
- `state`: (Conditionally required) If a `state` parameter was present in the request, then it must be returned in the response

An example authorization response for our application looks like this:

```
http://wmiig.com/callback?
    code=ey6XeGlAMHBpFi2LQ9JHyT6xwLbMxYRvyZAR
```

Given this response, we can extract the authorization code from the query component. Next, we must make another request to Facebook to exchange this for a valid access token.

> **Important notes about the authorization code**
>
> Recall from *Chapter 2, A Bird's Eye View of OAuth 2.0*, the authorization code that you receive here is consumable. That is, it can be exchanged for an access token only once. Any requests to exchange the same authorization code for a new access token will fail.
>
> Also, these codes typically have a short expiry time. For security purposes, they are meant to be used immediately after the client receives it. In fact, the OAuth 2.0 specification recommends that service providers limit the lifetime of their issued authorization codes to 10 minutes.

Error

If, however, the authorization response gets rejected for some reason, an error response will be returned. The properties for this error response are identical to the properties that can be returned for the implicit grant flow error response, except this response will be returned in the query component instead of the fragment. The template for this response is:

```
HTTP/1.1 302 Found
Location: [REDIRECT_URI]?
    error=[ERROR_CODE]&
    error_description=[ERROR_DESCRIPTION]&
    error_uri=[ERROR_URI]&
    state=[STATE]
```

The possible parameters that can be returned in this case are:

- `error`: (Required) This is a single code representing the error that caused the request to fail. The value must be one of the following:
    - `invalid_request`: The request is malformed and could not be processed.
    - `unauthorized_client`: The client application isn't authorized to make such a request.
    - `access_denied`: The user has denied the request.
    - `unsupported_response_type`: An invalid response type was used. Recall from earlier that for the authorization code grant type, this value must be set to `code`.
    - `invalid_scope`: The scope passed in is invalid.
    - `server_error`: An error happened on the server that prevented a successful response from being generated.
    - `temporarily_unavailable`: The authorization server is temporarily unavailable.
- `error_description`: (Optional) A human-readable message describing what caused the error.
- `error_uri`: (Optional) A link to a web document containing more information about the error.
- `state`: (Conditionally required) If a `state` parameter was present in the request, then it must be returned in the response.

An example response for our application, given the values we sent in the request, would be:

```
http://wmiig.com/callback?
    error=invalid_request&
    error_description=Unrecognized%20redirect%20URI
```

Here we can see that the error is `invalid_request` and the description (after URL-decoding) is "Unrecognized redirect URI". If you see something like this, make sure to check that you've properly whitelisted your redirection endpoint in your client configuration with the service provider.

Access token request

At this point, we have an authorization code, but not yet an access token. We have one more call to make to "exchange" our authorization code for an access token. Let's take a look at this process now.

According to the specification

In order to exchange our authorization code for an access token, we must make a `POST` request to the service provider's token endpoint, passing along a certain set of parameters. The parameters must be encoded using the `application/x-www-form-urlencoded` format. In general terms, the template for the access token request is:

```
POST /token HTTP/1.1
Host: server.example.com
Authorization: Basic [ENCODED_CLIENT_CREDENTIALS]
Content-Type: application/x-www-form-urlencoded

grant_type=authorization_code&
    code=[AUTHORIZATION_CODE]&
    redirect_uri=[REDIRECT_URI]&
    client_id=[CLIENT_ID]
```

The parameters that can be added to the preceding request body are defined as:

- `grant_type`: (Required) This must be set to `authorization_code` to signify that we are requesting an access token in exchange for an authorization code
- `code`: (Required) This is the authorization code value that you received in response to the authorization request we made earlier
- `redirect_uri`: (Conditionally required) If the redirection endpoint was included in the authorization request, it must be included in the access token request as well
- `client_id`: (Required) This is your application's unique client ID

In addition to passing in these parameters to the access token request, the client application must also identify itself with the service provider. This is an added layer of security only necessary for trusted clients and is known as **client authentication**. It entails the secure transmission of the client credentials to the service provider for validation.

Get an Access Token with the Server-Side Flow

Although the OAuth 2.0 specification doesn't mandate any particular authentication scheme for client authentication, this is typically done using HTTP basic authentication [RFC 2617]. This is represented by the `Authorization` header in the previous request template. What follows is a string representing the type of scheme, in this case "Basic", followed by the client credentials encoded according to the HTTP basic authentication scheme. Simply put, it is the Base64-encoded value of your client credentials in the form:

```
[CLIENT_ID]:[CLIENT_SECRET]
```

> **The HTTP basic access authentication protocol**
>
> The basic access authentication protocol, otherwise known as "basic auth" for short, is a means for an HTTP client to provide credentials (for example, username and password, or in our case, client ID and client secret) when making a request.
>
> For a link to more information on the basic auth scheme, see RFC 2617 in *Appendix C, Reference Specifications*.

> **In the real world**
>
> Although this behavior is described and recommended by the OAuth 2.0 specification, there are many service providers that do not support this. There are a variety of reasons for this, but perhaps the most common is that many companies started integrating with OAuth 2.0 long before the specification was ratified. Because of this, there were changes made to the specification that weren't (yet) implemented by their respective development teams.
>
> In the final specification, the client application identifies itself by passing in an authorization header using the basic auth protocol, containing its client ID and secret, as described earlier. However, before this change was made, the client secret was passed as a query parameter to the server itself, not making use of basic auth at all.
>
> You will find mixed adoption of both of these mechanisms. Some service providers will support the final version of the spec, and will honor the authorization header. Others only support the legacy mechanism and expect the client secret to be passed in explicitly in the request. You will have to experiment with the service you are trying to integrate with. Explore their documentation and experiment to see which methods they support.

For the sake of OAuth 2.0 service providers that don't support the latest recommended auth scheme (that is, using basic auth and the authorization header), let's also take a look at the legacy method. Knowing both of these should cover the majority of OAuth 2.0 service providers out there. In order to exchange an authorization code for an access token using the legacy method, we still make a `POST` request to the server as before. But this time, instead of passing in our client ID and client secret using the basic auth protocol, we will pass them in as parameters in the request body instead. The request structure for this now looks like:

```
POST /token HTTP/1.1
Host: server.example.com
Content-Type: application/x-www-form-urlencoded

grant_type=authorization_code&
    code=[AUTHORIZATION_CODE]&
    redirect_uri=[REDIRECT_URI]&
    client_id=[CLIENT_ID]&
    client_secret=[CLIENT_SECRET]
```

Notice that there is no more authorization header in this request, and now the client secret is passed in as a parameter in addition to the client ID in the request body. If you find that the service provider you are integrating with does not support the passing of your client credentials using basic auth, you may want to try this legacy method instead.

In our application

To make the access token request as described earlier, let's form our `POST` request accordingly. Given the description, our access token request will look like this:

```
POST /oauth/access_token HTTP/1.1
Host: graph.facebook.com
Authorization: Basic czZCaGRSa3F0MzpnWDFmQmF0M2JW
Content-Type: application/x-www-form-urlencoded

grant_type=authorization_code&code=SplxlOBeZQQYbYS6WxSbIA
&redirect_uri=http%3A%2F%2Fwmiig.com%2Fcallback
```

For legacy clients that don't support the passing of client credentials via basic auth, this same request would look like this:

```
POST /oauth/access_token HTTP/1.1
Host: graph.facebook.com
```

```
Content-Type: application/x-www-form-urlencoded

grant_type=authorization_code&code=SplxlOBeZQQYbYS6WxSbIA
&redirect_uri=http%3A%2F%2Fwmiig.com%2Fcallback
client_id=wmiig-23432&client_secret=DFIAJAO98SH9832HVMQI3
```

Access token response

If we made our access token request correctly and our authorization code is valid, we can expect an access token in our response. Otherwise, we will get an error response instead.

Success

If our access token request was successful, the following parameters will be sent back in the entity-body of the response:

- `access_token`: (Required) This is what we're after! The presence of this value in the response is indicative of a successful authorization and access token request. And it is this token value that we will eventually use to access the user's profile and feed data.

- `token_type`: (Required) Defines the type of token returned. This will almost always be `bearer`.

- `expires_in`: (Optional) The lifetime of the token in seconds. For example, if this value is 3600, that means that the access token will expire one hour from the time the response message was generated. It is optional in that the service provider may not always return this value.

- `refresh_token`: (Optional) This token may be used to refresh your access token in case it expires. Recall from the *Sometimes a refresh token* section in *Chapter 3, Four Easy Steps*, that depending on your service provider, this refresh token may or may not be returned. Refer to your service provider's documentation to see if they support the refresh token workflow.

- `scope`: (Conditionally required) If the granted scope is identical to what was requested, this value may be omitted. However, if the granted scope is different from the requested scope, it must be present.

An example access token response for our application may look like this:

```
HTTP/1.1 200 OK
Content-Type: application/json;charset=UTF-8
Cache-Control: no-store
Pragma: no-cache

{
  "access_token":"2YotnFZFEjr1zCsicMWpAA",
  "token_type":"bearer",
  "expires_in":3600,
  "refresh_token":"tGzv3JOkF0XG5Qx2TlKWIA",
}
```

Notice in this example, the response parameters are returned in the JSON format. However, your service provider may return it in other formats as well, such as XML or even key-value pairs in plaintext. Refer to your service provider's documentation for their supported access token response formats.

Error

If your access token request gets rejected for any reason, an access token will not be returned. Instead, the server will respond with an HTTP 400 (Bad Request) status code, including the following parameters in the body:

- error: (Required) This is a single code representing the error that caused the request to fail. The value must be one of the following:
    - invalid_request: The request is malformed and could not be processed
    - invalid_client: Client authentication failed
    - invalid_grant: The provided grant was invalid
    - unauthorized_client: The client application isn't authorized to make such a request
    - unsupported_grant_type: The authorization grant type is not supported
    - invalid_scope: The scope passed in is invalid
- error_description: (Optional) A human-readable message describing what caused the error.
- error_uri: (Optional) A link to a web document containing more information about the error.

An example response for our application might be:

```
HTTP/1.1 400 Bad Request
Content-Type: application/json;charset=UTF-8
Cache-Control: no-store
Pragma: no-cache

{
  "error":"invalid_client"
}
```

Here, we can see that we got an `invalid_client` error. If you get this error, you may want to check that your client credentials have been passed correctly.

Let's build it!

We have all the theory now. We know how to make the authorization request and the subsequent access token request, and we know the two types of responses we can get (success or error) for each one. Let's build it in our sample application!

Build the base application

To demonstrate the authorization code grant flow, we will be building a basic Java application. It will contain a simple HTML/JS frontend powered by a Java backend, which we will use to make our requests and process the responses. As we did in the previous chapter, we will also be using Apache Maven to facilitate the creation and running of this sample application. Many of these beginning steps for setting up the application are very similar to the steps we followed in the previous chapter. Some are even identical. After we have built the base application, though, the steps become quite different.

Install Apache Maven

If you haven't already installed Apache Maven for the sample application in the previous chapter, you will want to install it now. To download Maven, go to the official Apache Maven website, `https://maven.apache.org/`.

Download the latest version and follow the instructions to install it on your particular system. By the end of your installation, you should be able to execute the following command in a terminal on your machine and get a similar result:

Maven is now installed on your machine! Now, you're ready to start building the base application.

Create the project

Our base application for our server-side example will start with a simple JSP page. We can create this, along with the base application to house that JSP page, via Maven. Simply open up a terminal, navigate to the folder in which you want your project to live, and execute the following Maven command on your machine (note that this is the same Maven command we used in the last chapter to create our starter project):

```
mvn archetype:generate
     -DgroupId=com.wmiig
     -DartifactId=wmiig
     -DarchetypeArtifactId=maven-archetype-webapp
     -DinteractiveMode=false
```

Get an Access Token with the Server-Side Flow

Maven will do a bunch of work (less this time if you already executed this in the previous chapter), and at the end will create a folder called `wmiig`:

> If you created the sample project from the previous chapter, you may already have a `wmiig` folder. If so, you will either want to move the client-side version out of the way by renaming it to something else. Or, you could choose to rename this project folder instead. You can do this by simply changing the `artifactId` value.

This is where all of your project files are located. The directory structure of the files created is:

```
wmiig/
├── src/
│   └── main/
│       ├── resources/
│       └── webapp/
│           └── WEB-INF/
│               ├── web.xml
│               └── index.jsp
└── pom.xml
```

[98]

Configure the base project to fit our application

The application that has been created is very near where we want to be for our base application. We only have to make two simple changes.

First, let's replace the contents of `index.jsp` with:

```
<%@page language="java"
    contentType="text/html; charset=ISO-8859-1"
    pageEncoding="ISO-8859-1"%>
<!DOCTYPE html>
<html>
  <head>
    <title>The World's Most Interesting Infographic</title>
    <script src="//code.jquery.com/jquery-1.11.3.min.js"></script>
    <script>
      $(document).ready(function() {
        $("#goButton").click(makeRequest);
      });

      function makeRequest() {
        // TODO: Make authorization request
        alert("Button clicked!");
      }
    </script>
  </head>
  <body>
    <button id="goButton" type="button">Go!</button>
    <div id="results"></div>
  </body>
</html>
```

This is the same starter code we used in the implicit grant example, except as a JSP page instead of an HTML page.

Second, we need to include the necessary libraries that we will be using in our application. In this case, we will be including two dependencies: the Java Servlet API to handle our servlet definitions and mappings, and the Apache HTTP Client library to make our HTTP authorization and access token requests. To add these dependencies, open up the `pom.xml` file located at the project root and add the following snippets inside of the `dependencies` tag:

```xml
<dependencies>

  ...

  <dependency>
    <groupId>javax.servlet</groupId>
    <artifactId>servlet-api</artifactId>
    <version>2.5</version>
    <scope>provided</scope>
  </dependency>
  <dependency>
    <groupId>org.apache.httpcomponents</groupId>
    <artifactId>httpclient</artifactId>
    <version>4.5.1</version>
  </dependency>

  ...

</dependencies>
```

Modify the hosts file

This step is identical to the *Modify hosts file* step in the previous chapter, so if you've already done it, then you can skip this step entirely. If not, open up your `hosts` file on your machine and make sure the following entry is in place:

```
127.0.0.1 wmiig.com
```

With this entry in place, you can now refer to `localhost` using the hostname `wmiig.com`.

Running it for the first time

This step is also identical to what we did in the previous chapter. To run our server-side application for the first time, execute the following command in the same directory of your project:

```
sudo mvn -Dmaven.tomcat.port=80 -Dmaven.tomcat.path=/ tomcat:run
```

You should see the output similar to this:

Open up your favorite web browser, navigate to http://wmiig.com, and you should see a page that looks like this:

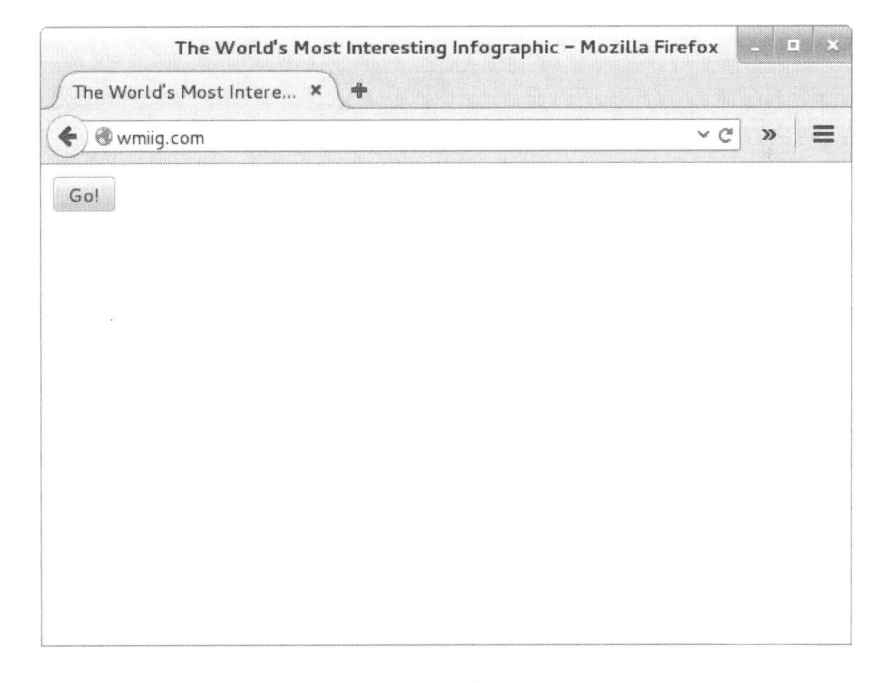

Success! If you click the button, you will see an alert that announces **Button clicked!** As we can see, our base application is functionally the same as the base application in the previous chapter. It is simply a basic JSP page containing an HTML button that, when clicked, pops up an alert announcing the click. Now, it is time to replace that alert with the actual authorization request to Facebook.

Make the authorization request

As we established earlier in the chapter, we must send the user-agent to:

```
https://www.facebook.com/dialog/oauth?
   response_type=code&
   client_id=wmiig-550106&
   redirect_uri=http%3A%2F%wmiig.com%2Fcallback&
   scope=public_profile%20user_posts
```

Let's do this in our application by replacing our `makeRequest()` function with this:

```
function makeRequest() {
  // Define properties
  var AUTH_ENDPOINT = "https://www.facebook.com/dialog/oauth";
  var RESPONSE_TYPE = "code";
  var CLIENT_ID = "wmiig-550106";
  var REDIRECT_URI = "http://wmiig.com/callback";
  var SCOPE = "public_profile user_posts";

  // Build authorization request endpoint
  var requestEndpoint = AUTH_ENDPOINT + "?" +
    "response_type=" + encodeURIComponent(RESPONSE_TYPE) + "&" +
    "client_id=" + encodeURIComponent(CLIENT_ID) + "&" +
    "redirect_uri=" + encodeURIComponent(REDIRECT_URI) + "&" +
    "scope=" + encodeURIComponent(SCOPE);

  // Send to authorization request endpoint
  window.location.href = requestEndpoint;
}
```

Notice, only two things have changed in this function compared with our client-side example: we changed the `response_type` value from `token` to `code`, and we are now using a different redirection endpoint.

Save your changes, restart your server, and reload the page. Now when you click "**Go!**", you will be taken to the user consent screen where you will be asked to authorize permission for WMIIG to access your public profile and feed data.

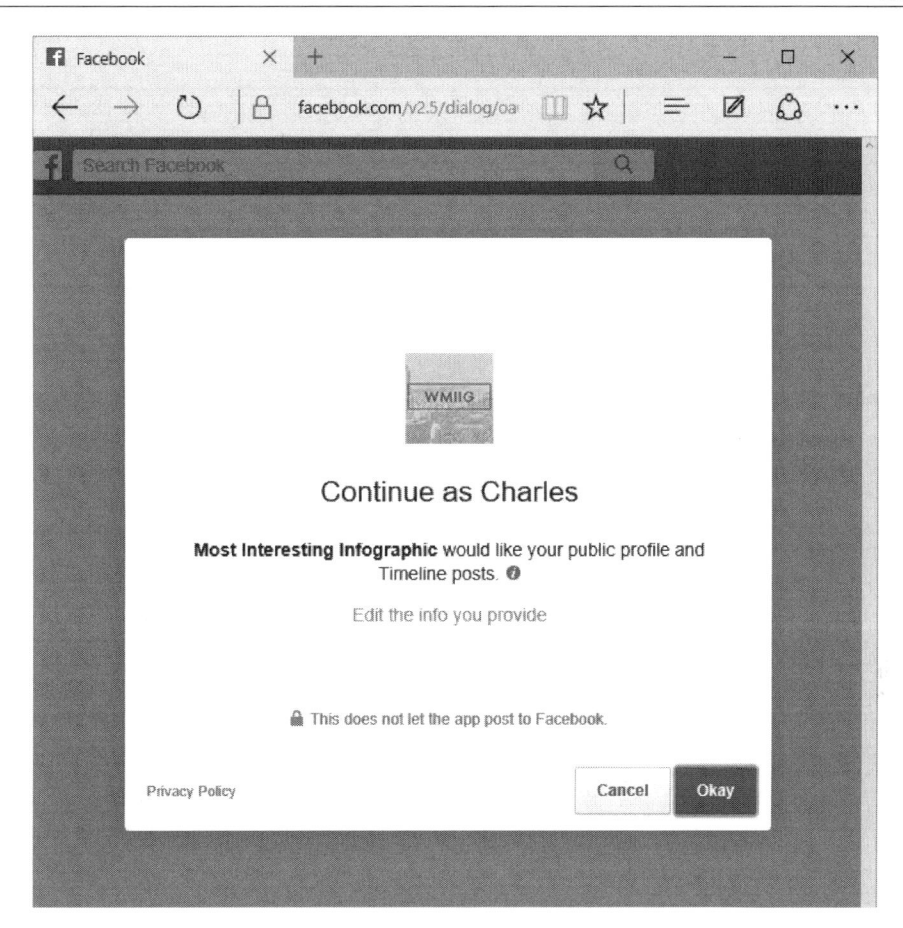

> **Going straight to an error page?**
>
> If you've already authorized the application in Facebook, say, in the previous chapter, then you won't be presented with the user consent screen again. Rather, Facebook will recognize that you've already authorized the application and immediately return an authorization code. You can verify this by inspecting the URL in your browser now. If it is your redirection endpoint followed by a query component, it means that you're on the right track. Just keep following along.
>
> If, however, you would like to see the user consent screen again, you will need to revoke the permissions that you have already granted to your application. To do this, you will have to visit the Facebook App Settings page (at the time of this writing, located at `https://www.facebook.com/settings?tab=applications`) and remove your application. Now, the next time you authorize within your application, you will be presented with the user consent screen.

So far so good! If you accept or deny the request, you will see an error page. This is because we specified our redirection endpoint as `http://wmiig.com/callback`, but we haven't yet created that page yet. Let's do this now.

Handle the authorization response

Once the user accepts the permissions requested in the user consent screen, an authorization code will be sent to the redirect URI of our server. We specified our redirect URI as `http://wmiig.com/callback`. We must make sure that we have that endpoint available on our server and "listening" for this response. To do this, we will create a servlet to listen at that endpoint.

To create our callback servlet, let's create a new Java file called `OAuthCallbackListener.java` and place it in the following location (you will need to create the necessary folders on the way to creating the file): `/src/main/java/com/wmiig/servlet`.

Fill the file with the following content:

```
package com.wmiig.servlet;

import java.io.IOException;
import javax.servlet.ServletException;
import javax.servlet.http.HttpServlet;
import javax.servlet.http.HttpServletRequest;
import javax.servlet.http.HttpServletResponse;

public class OAuthCallbackListener extends HttpServlet {
  private static final long serialVersionUID = 1L;

  protected void doGet(HttpServletRequest request,
    HttpServletResponse response) throws ServletException,
    IOException {
    // TODO: Detect presence of an authorization code
  }
}
```

This class serves as the servlet definition. Now, we have to wire it up in our application to have it listen at a particular endpoint, in our case `/callback`. To do this, open up the `web.xml` file located at `/src/main/webapp/WEB-INF` and place the following snippet somewhere between the `web-app` tags:

```xml
<web-app>

  ...

  <servlet>
    <servlet-name>OAuthCallbackListener</servlet-name>
    <servlet-class>
        com.wmiig.servlet.OAuthCallbackListener
    </servlet-class>
  </servlet>
  <servlet-mapping>
    <servlet-name>OAuthCallbackListener</servlet-name>
    <url-pattern>/callback</url-pattern>
  </servlet-mapping>

  ...

</web-app>
```

Once we've done this, we should now have a servlet "listening" at this `/callback` endpoint. But right now it doesn't do anything! Let's make it accept the response, look for the authorization code, and if present, exchange it for an access token. First, let's make it detect the presence of an authorization code.

Let's replace the empty `doGet()` method with:

```java
protected void doGet(HttpServletRequest request,
    HttpServletResponse response) throws ServletException,
    IOException {

  // Detect the presence of an authorization code
  String authorizationCode = request.getParameter("code");
  if (authorizationCode != null && authorizationCode.length() > 0) {
    // TODO: Exchange authorization code for access token
  } else {
    // Handle failure
  }

}
```

Good! Now, we can detect when we have an authorization code. Let's now exchange it for an access token by making our access token request.

Make the access token request

Once the server has the authorization code, all that is left is to "exchange" this for an access token. As we mentioned earlier in the chapter, this must be done with a `POST` request to the service provider's token endpoint, passing a certain set of parameters in the request body as well as an authorization header containing our client credentials encoded using the basic auth protocol. Once again, the template for such a request is:

```
POST /token HTTP/1.1
Host: server.example.com
Authorization: Basic [ENCODED_CLIENT_CREDENTIALS]
Content-Type: application/x-www-form-urlencoded

grant_type=authorization_code&
    code=[AUTHORIZATION_CODE]&
    redirect_uri=[REDIRECT_URI]&
    client_id=[CLIENT_ID]
```

We can make such a request using the Apache HTTP Client with the following snippet:

```java
import java.net.URLEncoder;
import java.nio.charset.StandardCharsets;

import org.apache.commons.codec.binary.Base64;
import org.apache.http.HttpResponse;
import org.apache.http.client.methods.HttpPost;
import org.apache.http.impl.client.CloseableHttpClient;
import org.apache.http.impl.client.HttpClients;

...

final String TOKEN_ENDPOINT =
  "https://graph.facebook.com/oauth/access_token";
final String GRANT_TYPE = "authorization_code";
final String REDIRECT_URI = "http://wmiig.com/callback";
final String CLIENT_ID = "wmiig-550106";
final String CLIENT_SECRET = "DFIAJAO98SH9832HVMQI3";

// Generate POST request
HttpPost httpPost = new HttpPost(TOKEN_ENDPOINT +
  "?grant_type=" + URLEncoder.encode(GRANT_TYPE,
  StandardCharsets.UTF_8.name()) +
  "&code=" + URLEncoder.encode(authorizationCode,
  StandardCharsets.UTF_8.name()) +
```

```
    "&redirect_uri=" + URLEncoder.encode(REDIRECT_URI,
    StandardCharsets.UTF_8.name()) +
    "&client_id=" + URLEncoder.encode(CLIENT_ID,
    StandardCharsets.UTF_8.name()));

// Add "Authorization" header with encoded client credentials
String clientCredentials = CLIENT_ID + ":" + CLIENT_SECRET;
String encodedClientCredentials =
  new String(Base64.encodeBase64(clientCredentials.getBytes()));
httpPost.setHeader("Authorization", "Basic " +
  encodedClientCredentials);

// Make the access token request
CloseableHttpClient httpClient = HttpClients.createDefault();
HttpResponse httpResponse = httpClient.execute(httpPost);

// TODO: Handle access token response

httpClient.close();
```

We will want to place this code where we have detected the presence of the authorization code. Doing so, our new doGet() method now looks like this:

```
protected void doGet(HttpServletRequest request,
    HttpServletResponse response) throws ServletException,
    IOException {

  // Detect the presence of an authorization code
  String authorizationCode = request.getParameter("code");
  if (authorizationCode != null && authorizationCode.length() > 0)
  {
    final String TOKEN_ENDPOINT =
      "https://graph.facebook.com/oauth/access_token";
    final String GRANT_TYPE = "authorization_code";
    final String REDIRECT_URI = "http://wmiig.com/callback";
    final String CLIENT_ID = "wmiig-550106";
    final String CLIENT_SECRET = "DFIAJAO98SH9832HVMQI3";

    // Generate POST request
    HttpPost httpPost = new HttpPost(TOKEN_ENDPOINT +
      "?grant_type=" + URLEncoder.encode(GRANT_TYPE,
      StandardCharsets.UTF_8.name()) +
      "&code=" + URLEncoder.encode(authorizationCode,
      StandardCharsets.UTF_8.name()) +
      "&redirect_uri=" + URLEncoder.encode(REDIRECT_URI,
      StandardCharsets.UTF_8.name()) +
      "&client_id=" + URLEncoder.encode(CLIENT_ID,
      StandardCharsets.UTF_8.name()));
```

```java
      // Add "Authorization" header with encoded client credentials
      String clientCredentials = CLIENT_ID + ":" + CLIENT_SECRET;
      String encodedClientCredentials =
        new String(Base64.encodeBase64(clientCredentials.getBytes()));
      httpPost.setHeader("Authorization", "Basic " +
        encodedClientCredentials);

      // Make the access token request
      CloseableHttpClient httpClient = HttpClients.createDefault();
      HttpResponse httpResponse = httpClient.execute(httpPost);

      // TODO: Handle access token response

      httpClient.close();
    } else {
      // Handle failure
    }

}
```

Handle the access token response

We're almost there. At this point, we've made the authorization request, detected the presence of an authorization code in the response, and now we're making the access token request using the authorization code we received. Finally, we have to parse the access token from the access token response. This is easy since we are using the Apache HTTP Client. Once we've made the request, we can parse the access token from the response with the following code:

```java
import java.io.BufferedReader;
import java.io.InputStreamReader;
import java.io.Reader;

...

// Handle access token response
Reader reader = new
  InputStreamReader(httpResponse.getEntity().getContent());
BufferedReader bufferedReader = new BufferedReader(reader);
String line = bufferedReader.readLine();

// Isolate access token
String accessToken = null;
String[] responseProperties = line.split("&");
for (String responseProperty : responseProperties) {
  if (responseProperty.startsWith("access_token=")) {
```

```
        accessToken = responseProperty.split("=")[1];
        break;
      }
    }

    // TODO: Request profile and feed data with access token
    System.out.println("Access token: " + accessToken);
```

Your final `OAuthCallbackListener.java` class should now look like this:

```
package com.wmiig.servlet;

import java.io.BufferedReader;
import java.io.IOException;
import java.io.InputStreamReader;
import java.io.Reader;
import java.net.URLEncoder;
import java.nio.charset.StandardCharsets;

import javax.servlet.ServletException;
import javax.servlet.http.HttpServlet;
import javax.servlet.http.HttpServletRequest;
import javax.servlet.http.HttpServletResponse;

import org.apache.commons.codec.binary.Base64;
import org.apache.http.HttpResponse;
import org.apache.http.client.methods.HttpPost;
import org.apache.http.impl.client.CloseableHttpClient;
import org.apache.http.impl.client.HttpClients;

public class OAuthCallbackListener extends HttpServlet {
    private static final long serialVersionUID = 1L;
    protected void doGet(HttpServletRequest request,
        HttpServletResponse response) throws ServletException,
        IOException {

      // Detect the presence of an authorization code
      String authorizationCode = request.getParameter("code");
      if (authorizationCode != null && authorizationCode.length() > 0) {

        final String TOKEN_ENDPOINT =
          "https://graph.facebook.com/oauth/access_token";
        final String GRANT_TYPE = "authorization_code";
        final String REDIRECT_URI = "http://wmiig.com/callback";
        final String CLIENT_ID = "wmiig-550106";
        final String CLIENT_SECRET = "DFIAJAO98SH9832HVMQI3";
```

```java
        // Generate POST request
        HttpPost httpPost = new HttpPost(TOKEN_ENDPOINT +
          "?grant_type=" + URLEncoder.encode(GRANT_TYPE,
          StandardCharsets.UTF_8.name()) +
          "&code=" + URLEncoder.encode(authorizationCode,
          StandardCharsets.UTF_8.name()) +
          "&redirect_uri=" + URLEncoder.encode(REDIRECT_URI,
          StandardCharsets.UTF_8.name()) +
          "&client_id=" + URLEncoder.encode(CLIENT_ID,
          StandardCharsets.UTF_8.name()));

        // Add "Authorization" header with encoded client credentials
        String clientCredentials = CLIENT_ID + ":" + CLIENT_SECRET;
        String encodedClientCredentials =
          new String(Base64.encodeBase64
            (clientCredentials.getBytes()));
        httpPost.setHeader("Authorization", "Basic " +
          encodedClientCredentials);

        // Make the access token request
        CloseableHttpClient httpClient =
          HttpClients.createDefault();
        HttpResponse httpResponse = httpClient.execute(httpPost);

        // Handle access token response
        Reader reader = new InputStreamReader
          (httpResponse.getEntity().getContent());
        BufferedReader bufferedReader = new BufferedReader(reader);
        String line = bufferedReader.readLine();

        // Isolate access token
        String accessToken = null;
        String[] responseProperties = line.split("&");
        for (String responseProperty : responseProperties) {
          if (responseProperty.startsWith("access_token=")) {
            accessToken = responseProperty.split("=")[1];
            break;
          }
        }

        // TODO: Request profile and feed data with access token
        System.out.println("Access token: " + accessToken);

        httpClient.close();
      } else {
        // Handle failure
      }
    }
  }
}
```

Save your changes, restart your server, and reload the page once again. This time, when you click on **Go!**, the application will make the access token request and, if successful, print it to your console:

```
Mercury:wmiig charles$ sudo mvn -Dmaven.tomcat.port=80 -Dmaven.tomcat.path=/ tomcat:run
[INFO] Scanning for projects...
[INFO]
[INFO] ------------------------------------------------------------------------
[INFO] Building wmiig Maven Webapp 1.0-SNAPSHOT
[INFO] ------------------------------------------------------------------------
[INFO]
[INFO] >>> tomcat-maven-plugin:1.1:run (default-cli) > compile @ wmiig >>>
[INFO]
[INFO] --- maven-resources-plugin:2.6:resources (default-resources) @ wmiig ---
[WARNING] Using platform encoding (UTF-8 actually) to copy filtered resources, i.e. build is platform dependent!
[INFO] Copying 0 resource
[INFO]
[INFO] --- maven-compiler-plugin:3.1:compile (default-compile) @ wmiig ---
[INFO] Nothing to compile - all classes are up to date
[INFO]
[INFO] <<< tomcat-maven-plugin:1.1:run (default-cli) < compile @ wmiig <<<
[INFO]
[INFO] --- tomcat-maven-plugin:1.1:run (default-cli) @ wmiig ---
[INFO] Running war on http://localhost:80/
[INFO] Using existing Tomcat server configuration at /Users/charles/wmiig/target/tomcat
Nov 07, 2015 8:53:02 PM org.apache.catalina.startup.Embedded start
INFO: Starting tomcat server
Nov 07, 2015 8:53:03 PM org.apache.catalina.core.StandardEngine start
INFO: Starting Servlet Engine: Apache Tomcat/6.0.29
Nov 07, 2015 8:53:03 PM org.apache.coyote.http11.Http11Protocol init
INFO: Initializing Coyote HTTP/1.1 on http-80
Nov 07, 2015 8:53:03 PM org.apache.coyote.http11.Http11Protocol start
INFO: Starting Coyote HTTP/1.1 on http-80
Access token: CAAEvZCNK2AWsBADAvUXE343iyrhKtyTn70eX8wLoxDP1rN83gYEkkWyAHXKAgO6ZAMQOqhumN9La1VGIc50z1gXfJoQrjlVNf
fDbRgHkw4qD0E3zEjuZB8YDmbNeqDiZBUlyw6j98PaNQ9Oz3zljnF0GS8fgDeOD10Y5sGw3KYdZChAqAbqPhAaPrf4vUbtedk6WEPwC6hgZDZD
```

That's it! We now have an access token! In the next chapter, we move on to actually using this access token to request permission to access a protected resource.

Summary

We accomplished a lot in this chapter. We explored the authorization code grant flow, noting differences with the implicit grant flow, which we demonstrated in the previous chapter. During this detailed exploration of the protocol, we discussed the traits of the flow that make it more secure and the preferred authorization flow for OAuth 2.0 clients. We also saw how some service providers may not necessarily abide by the final version of the OAuth 2.0 specification. To remedy this, we explored some alternative methods for gaining authorization and fetching tokens that were supported in previous versions of the specification. It all culminated when we created a simple Java application to request an access token from Facebook for our sample application, *The World's Most Interesting Infographic Generator*. Next, we will be looking at how to use this newly obtained access token to request access to our user's profile and feed data.

Reference pages

Use these pages as reference documentation when implementing the authorization code grant flow in your application. Adapted from *The OAuth 2.0 Authorization Framework* specification [RFC 6749].

An overview of the authorization code grant flow

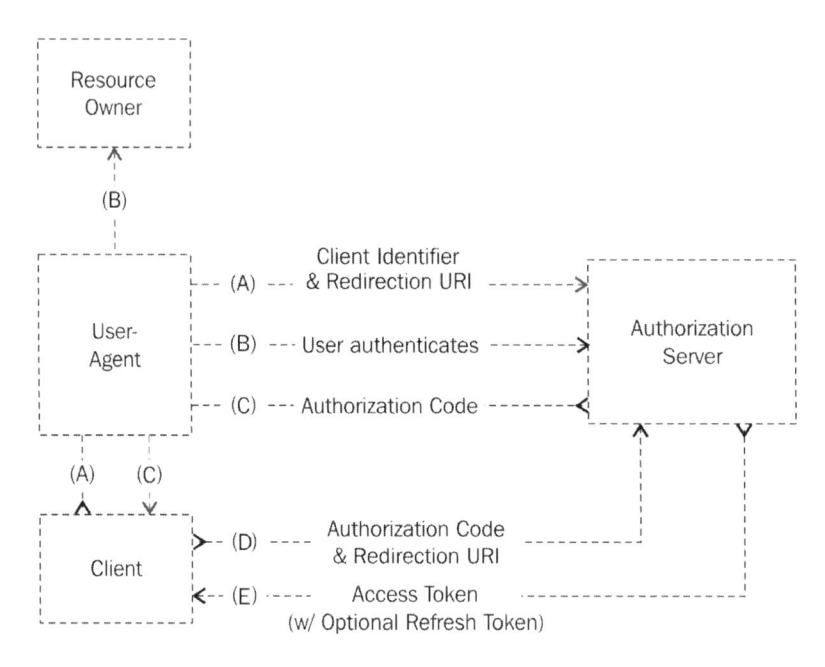

Figure 3 from RFC 6749

The steps are as follows:

- **A**: The client application initiates the flow by sending the user's user-agent to the appropriate authorization endpoint.
- **B**: The authentication server of the service provider authenticates the resource owner and attempts to gain consent by presenting the user consent form.
- **C**: Assuming the user grants consent, the authorization server redirects the user back to the client application via the redirection endpoint provided in the authorization request. The redirection endpoint will include an authorization code and any state provided by the client.
- **D**: The client requests an access token from the service provider's token endpoint by including the authorization code received in the previous step. When making this request, the client also authenticates with the service provider by passing its client credentials with the request.
- **E**: The service provider authenticates the client, validates the authorization code, and ensures that the redirection URI received matches the URI used to redirect the client in step (C). If valid, the authorization server responds with an access token and, optionally, a refresh token.

Authorization request

The client constructs the authorization request endpoint by appending the following properties to the query component of the service provider's authorization endpoint. All property values must be encoded using the `application/x-www-form-urlencoded` format, as described in Appendix B of the specification:

- `response_type`: (Required) Value must be set to `code`.
- `client_id`: (Required) A unique string representing the client as was provided during client registration.
- `redirect_uri`: (Optional) An absolute URI to be used to pass control back to the client after the service provider has completed interacting with the user.
- `scope`: (Optional) A list of space-delimited, case-sensitive strings which represent the scope of the access request.
- `state`: (Recommended) An opaque value used by the client to maintain state between the request and callback. This parameter should be used for the prevention of cross-site request forgery, as described in Section 10.12 of the specification.

An example authorization request looks like this:

```
GET /authorize?
  response_type=code&
  client_id=s6BhdRkqt3&state=xyz&
  redirect_uri=https%3A%2F%Eexample%2Ecom%2Fcallback HTTP/1.1
Host: server.example.com
```

Authorization response

If the user grants access for the protected resource to the client application, the success response will be sent to the client application in the query component of the redirect URI with the following properties encoded using the `application/x-www-form-urlencoded` format as described in Appendix B of the specification:

- `code`: (Required) The authorization code generated by the authorization server. This value must have a short lifetime, recommended as 10 minutes by the specification. Further, this code is restricted for a single use only. Any requests using the same code must be denied.
- `state`: (Conditionally required) An opaque value used by the client to maintain state between the request and callback. This parameter should be used for the prevention of cross-site request forgery, as described in Section 10.12 of the specification.

An example authorization response looks like this:

```
HTTP/1.1 302 Found
Location: https://example.com/callback?
    code=SplxlOBeZQQYbYS6WxSbIA&
    state=xyz
```

Error response

If the access request fails for any reason, the error response will be sent to the client application in the query component of the redirect URI with the following properties encoded using the `application/x-www-form-urlencoded` format as described in Appendix B of the specification:

- `error`: (Required) This is a single error code representing the condition that caused the request to fail. The value must be one of the following:
    - `invalid_request`: The request is missing a required parameter, includes an invalid parameter value, includes a parameter more than once, or is otherwise malformed.

- `unauthorized_client`: The client is not authorized to request an access token using this method.
- `access_denied`: The user or service provider denied the request.
- `unsupported_response_type`: The service provider does not support obtaining an access token using this method.
- `invalid_scope`: The requested scope is invalid, unknown, or malformed.
- `server_error`: The service provider encountered an unexpected error that prevented it from fulfilling the request. This error code is necessary because an HTTP 500 (Internal Server Error) status code cannot be returned to the client via an HTTP redirect.
- `temporarily_unavailable`: The authorization server is currently unable to handle the request. This error code is necessary because an HTTP 503 (Service Unavailable) status code cannot be returned to the client via an HTTP redirect.

- `error_description`: (Optional) Human-readable ASCII message providing additional information regarding the error.
- `error_uri`: (Optional) A URI identifying a human-readable web page providing additional information regarding the error.
- `state`: (Conditionally required) Required only if the `state` parameter was present in the authorization request. Must be the same value as was received by the client.

An example error response looks like this:

```
HTTP/1.1 302 Found
Location: https://example.com/callback?
  error=access_denied&
  state=xyz
```

Access token request

The client makes a POST request to the service provider's token endpoint, passing in the following parameters encoded using the `application/x-www-form-urlencoded` format, as described in Appendix B of the specification:

- `grant_type`: (Required) This value must be set to `authorization_code`
- `code`: (Required) The authorization code received from the service provider

- `redirect_uri`: (Conditionally required) Required only if the `redirect_uri` parameter was included in the authorization request, and their values must be identical
- `client_id`: (Conditionally required) Required only if the client is not authenticating with the authorization server, as described in Section 3.2.1 of the specification

As part of this request, the client application must also authenticate with the service provider. This is typically done using the HTTP basic authentication scheme [RFC 2617], but other authentication schemes may be supported by the service provider as well, such as HTTP digest authentication or public/private key authentication.

An example access token request using HTTP basic authentication looks like this:

```
POST /token HTTP/1.1
Host: server.example.com
Authorization: Basic czZCaGRSa3F0MzpnWDFmQmF0M2JW
Content-Type: application/x-www-form-urlencoded

grant_type=authorization_code&
  code=SplxlOBeZQQYbYS6WxSbIA&
  redirect_uri=https%3A%2F%2Fexample%2Ecom%2Fcallback
```

Access token response

If the access token request is valid and authorized, the response will contain an access token, optional refresh token, and other parameters, as described here:

- `access_token`: (Required) The access token issued by the service provider.
- `token_type`: (Required) The type of the token issued. This value is case-insensitive.
- `expires_in`: (Optional) The lifetime of the access token given in seconds. If omitted, the service provider should communicate the expiration time via other means.
- `refresh_token`: (Optional) A refresh token, which can be used to obtain new access tokens using the refresh token workflow.
- `scope`: (Conditionally required) A list of space-delimited, case-sensitive strings which represent the scope of the access granted. Required only if the scope granted is different from the scope requested.

An example access token response looks like this:

```
HTTP/1.1 200 OK
Content-Type: application/json;charset=UTF-8
Cache-Control: no-store
Pragma: no-cache

{
  "access_token":"2YotnFZFEjr1zCsicMWpAA",
  "token_type":"bearer",
  "expires_in":3600,
  "refresh_token":"tGzv3JOkF0XG5Qx2TlKWIA",
  "example_parameter":"example_value"
}
```

Error response

If the access token request fails for any reason, the server will respond with an HTTP 400 (Bad Request) status code including the following properties:

- `error`: (Required) This is a single error code representing the condition that caused the request to fail. The value must be one of the following:
    - `invalid_request`: The request is missing a required parameter, includes an unsupported parameter value (other than grant type), repeats a parameter, includes multiple credentials, utilizes more than one mechanism for authenticating the client, or is otherwise malformed
    - `invalid_client`: Client authentication failed for some reason (for example, unknown client, no client authentication included, or unsupported authentication method)
    - `invalid_grant`: The provided authorization grant or refresh token is invalid, expired, revoked, does not match the redirection URI used in the authorization request, or was issued to another client
    - `unauthorized_client`: The authenticated client is not authorized to use this authorization grant type
    - `unsupported_grant_type`: The authorization grant type is not supported by the authorization server
    - `invalid_scope`: The requested scope is invalid, unknown, malformed, or exceeds the scope granted by the user

- `error_description`: (Optional) Human-readable ASCII message providing additional information regarding the error.
- `error_uri`: (Optional) A URI identifying a human-readable web page providing additional information regarding the error.

An example error response looks like this:

```
HTTP/1.1 400 Bad Request
Content-Type: application/json;charset=UTF-8
Cache-Control: no-store
Pragma: no-cache
{
  "error":"invalid_request"
}
```

7
Use Your Access Token

Up until this point in the book, we have spent all of our energy trying to obtain an access token. In the previous two chapters, we were able to obtain access tokens using both the implicit grant flow for our client-side example, and the authorization code grant flow for our server-side example.

In this chapter, we will finally use the access token we've been working so hard to obtain. We will do so by requesting access to protected resources on the service provider. In particular, we will use this access token to make API calls to Facebook's Graph API to get data that we can use to build our infographic.

Refresher on access tokens

Recall from the *A closer look at access tokens* section in *Chapter 3*, *Four Easy Steps*, an access token is an opaque string given to clients that provides temporary access to a protected resource. More specifically, they represent a specific scope of permissions and duration of access for a particular client application to use, all of which are enforced by the service provider. This can be thought of simply as an encapsulation of the user's authorization to access or modify a particular scope of their resources.

Use your access token to make an API call

Now that we have the ability to fetch access tokens from the service provider using either the implicit grant flow or the authorization code grant flow, let's finally utilize these tokens to access protected resources. This is done via API calls to the service provider, in our case, Facebook. When making an API call to request access to a protected resource, the respective access token must be provided as well. This allows the service provider to validate the token by ensuring that the token has not expired or been revoked and that its associated scope covers the requested resource.

There are three prescribed methods for passing the access token in an API call. Those methods are:

- Authorization request header field
- Form-encoded body parameter
- URI query parameter

> **Only for bearer tokens!**
>
> These three methods are only for tokens of the type `bearer`, which is the only type of token we have dealt with in this book. However, there are other token types that can be used. For instance, `mac` tokens, and even proprietary tokens. For these types of tokens, you may need to use different methods for passing the access token to the service provider. You will need to refer to the documentation for the particular token type for more information on its usage.

These various methods allow the client to transmit the access token to the service provider for validation when requesting access to a resource. Each one has its own benefits and drawbacks. Also, certain service providers may only support a subset of these methods, so it is important to know each of them, and when it is appropriate to use them. Let's take a closer look at these methods.

The authorization request header field

This method for passing your access token to the service provider makes use of the `Authorization` header in your HTTP request. The value for this header is the token type followed by the token value. An example of this type of request looks like this:

```
GET /resource HTTP/1.1
Host: server.example.com
Authorization: Bearer mF_9.B5f-4.1JqM
```

Note that the syntax of this authentication scheme is similar to the basic authentication scheme we used in the previous chapter for the access token request, except that the authentication scheme is denoted by the term Bearer instead of Basic.

This method for passing your access token is preferred by the OAuth 2.0 specification. However, since this method requires HTTP header manipulation, it often isn't the easiest method to use during development and while debugging. Fortunately, other methods are available for this purpose.

The form-encoded body parameter

Another method for sending your access token to the service provider involves including and modifying different HTTP header fields other than the Authorization header field described in the previous section. For this method, we will make use of form-encoded body parameters. An example of this type of request looks like this:

```
POST /resource HTTP/1.1
Host: server.example.com
Content-Type: application/x-www-form-urlencoded

access_token=mF_9.B5f-4.1JqM
```

Note that this request is a POST request, not a GET request. Because we include the access token in the request body, some additional restrictions are in place to use this method:

- The Content-Type header must be present and set to application/x-www-form-urlencoded
- The request body must be URL-encoded using the application/x-www-form-urlencoded format

It is advisable that this method is used only when the authorization request header method is unavailable.

The URI query parameter

This final method for passing your access token to the service provider involves including it as a query parameter to your request URI. An example of this request would look like this:

```
GET /resource?access_token=mF_9.B5f-4.1JqM HTTP/1.1
Host: server.example.com
```

Use Your Access Token

This is a very simple approach and offers particular advantages for application developers. Namely, this approach doesn't require the manipulation of HTTP request headers, nor does it require the request method to be a POST. Because of these reasons, the URI query parameter method offers a very easy way to test and debug your application and access tokens. Rather than generating new requests programmatically, you can simply test your API calls directly by attaching your access token to the API endpoint.

However, this simplistic approach does have some important security implications. For instance, passing your access token via the URI has the high likelihood that the URI, along with your access token, will get logged at some point. Because of this significant security weakness associated with this method, it is typically only used for debugging purposes and should *not* be used for real production clients.

> **In the real world**
>
> You will typically use this method during development while debugging your applications. It is a quick and easy way to check your access tokens and API calls. You can simply enter your target URL directly in the browser and examine the results. However, once you move out of development, you should abandon this usage in your application and replace it with one of the previously mentioned, more secure methods.

Let's build it!

Now that we know more about access tokens, and the various ways to pass them along to the service provider during an API call, let's incorporate this into our application! Currently, we have two versions of our sample application: the client-side example and the server-side example. We will make API calls in both versions of the application, and we will look at utilizing all three methods of passing the access token. Let's begin!

> **The Facebook Graph API**
>
> For our sample application, we will be making API calls to Facebook's Graph API. This is the API that Facebook offers developers who want to integrate with their services. Protected and accessed using OAuth 2.0, this makes for an ideal setting to demonstrate our usage of the protocol. Find more information on the Facebook Graph API at `https://developers.facebook.com/docs/graph-api`.

In our client-side application

In *Chapter 5, Get an Access Token with the Client-Side Flow*, we built an HTML/JS webpage capable of requesting an access token from Facebook using the implicit grant flow via JavaScript. Now that we know how to fetch an access token, let's make an API call to Facebook's Graph API to request the user's profile information for us to use in our application.

Picking up where we last left our client-side application, we had just implemented the logic to make an authorization request using the implicit grant and receive an access token. The code to parse the response and extract the access token looks like this:

```
// Isolate access token and write it to the "response" div
var accessToken = "";
for (var i = 0; i < responseProperties.length; i++) {
  if (responseProperties[i].indexOf("access_token=") === 0) {
    accessToken = responseProperties[i].split("=")[1];
    $("#response").html("Access token: " + accessToken);
    break;
  }
}

// TODO: Request profile and feed data with access token
```

Now, instead of simply appending the access token to the response tag, let's actually make an API call to retrieve the user's profile data.

Referring to the API documentation provided by Facebook to fetch user information, we will want to use the `user` API. This can be accessed by hitting the following endpoint with a basic `GET` request at `https://graph.facebook.com/[API_VERSION]/me`.

This will return the profile data for the user who was granted access for the particular access token used in this request. We can include additional parameters to further restrict this call. For instance, rather than returning all of the default profile data, we're really only interested in the user's name (for now—you may want to use other data in the user profile). To restrict this, we will add the `fields` parameter, specifying only `name` as the profile field we're interested in: `https://graph.facebook.com/[API_VERSION]/me?fields=name`.

Now that we know the protected resource endpoint and the associated parameters we want to pass in, let's look at making this call to actually retrieve some profile data.

Send via the URI query parameter

Before we start coding the API call into our application, let's first test our API call assumptions. As we discussed earlier, we can easily test our API call and access token by using the URI query parameter method for passing the access token. Given the description of the user API and our knowledge of the URI query parameter method, the endpoint we will want to hit is (assuming v2.5 of the Facebook Graph API):

```
https://graph.facebook.com/v2.5/me?
    fields=name&
    access_token=[ACCESS_TOKEN_VALUE]
```

We can easily test this by plugging in an access token value that we've received in our client-side application and simply hitting this endpoint directly in a browser. If we did this correctly, and our access token was still valid, we should see something like this:

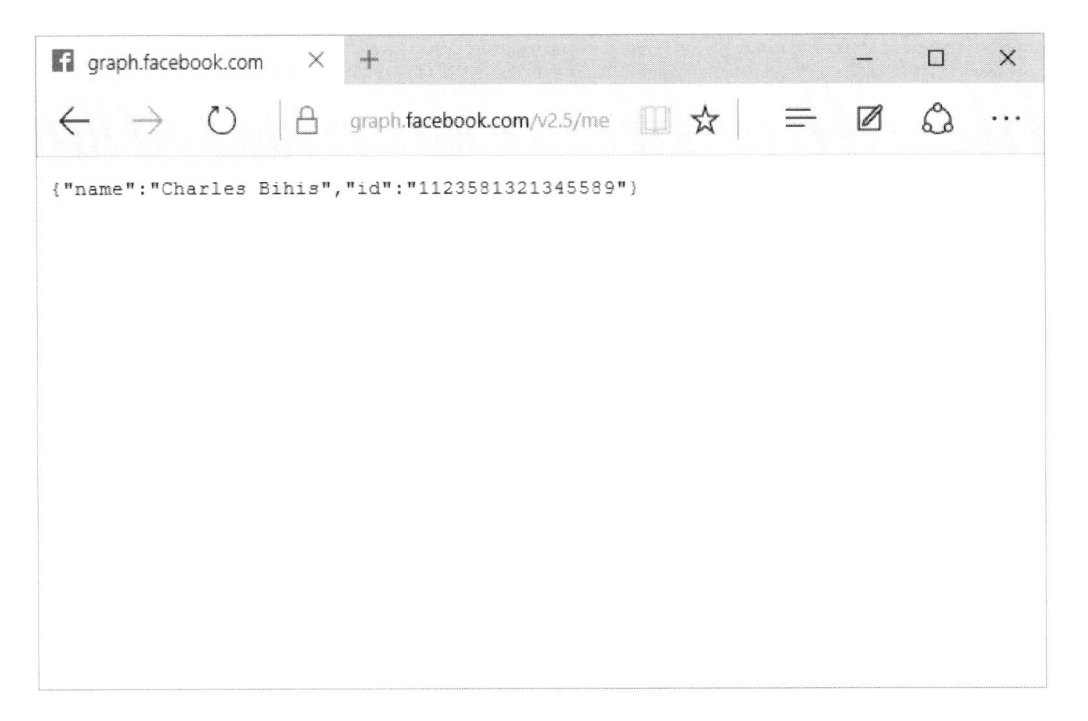

```
{"name":"Charles Bihis","id":"1123581321345589"}
```

As you can see, the simplicity of this method for passing in your access token provides a lot of convenience for application developers when testing their applications. Now that we have confirmed the behavior of the user API, let's actually make a proper request in our client-side application.

Send via the form-encoded body parameter

For the implementation of this `user` API call in our client-side application, let's use the form-encoded body parameter method. We can use the HTTP authorization header method but, just so we get the opportunity to explore each of the methods, let's save that for the server-side example which comes next.

For this request, we will be making a `POST` request to the `user` API, rather than a `GET` request, providing the `fields` parameter to restrict the fields returned. Instead of passing in the access token as a query parameter as we did for our preceding test request, this time we will add it to the request body as described by the form-encoded body parameter method. We can do this easily with jQuery using the following snippet:

```
// Request profile data with access token
$.ajax({  type: "POST",
  url: "https://graph.facebook.com/v2.5/me?fields=name",
  headers: {"Content-Type": "application/x-www-form-urlencoded"},
  data: {
    access_token: encodeURIComponent(accessToken),
    method: "get"
  },
  contentType: "application/x-www-form-urlencoded",
  success: function(data) {
    $("#response").html("Hello, " + data.name + "!");
  }
});
```

Notice that in the success handler, we handle the response and display a custom greeting message to our user. Let's see what that looks like.

Use Your Access Token

That's it! We've made our first successful API call using OAuth 2.0 in our application! Congratulations!

> **Check your work on GitHub!**
> All of the sample code used in this book is available for your reference on our public GitHub account! If you'd like to check your work, feel free to visit the GitHub page for this particular sample project, located at `https://github.com/mastering-oauth-2/client-side-example`.

In our server-side application

Now that we've seen how to use our access token to request profile data in our client-side application, let's take a look at how to do something similar in our server-side application. In the previous example, we invoked the `user` API to get the profile data for the logged-in user. This time, let's make a request to fetch the feed data for that user. We can then combine these two API calls to make the world's most interesting infographic!

Referring once again to the API documentation for the Facebook Graph API, in order to fetch the feed data for a user, we must invoke the `user feed` API. The endpoint for this resource is `https://graph.facebook.com/[API_VERSION]/me/feed`.

Just as we can pass in additional parameters to the `user` resource, we can do so with the `feed` resource too. This time, let's limit the number of posts to return by adding the `limit` parameter: `https://graph.facebook.com/[API_VERSION]/me/feed?limit=25`.

This restricts the response set to include only the user's most recent 25 posts. We can use the data from this result to glean all sorts of interesting insights that we can share with the user. Let's build it!

Send via the URI query parameter

As we did with our client-side example, let's look at how to make this API call using the URI query parameter method for the purpose of testing. The first thing we need to do is construct our request URL. Based on the documentation for the resource and our knowledge of the URI query parameter method, the endpoint we want to hit is (again, assuming v2.5 of the Facebook Graph API):

```
https://graph.facebook.com/v2.5/me/feed?
   limit=25&
   access_token=[ACCESS_TOKEN]
```

Instead of hitting this in a browser directly like we did in the previous section, let's use the cURL command instead (see the *Tools* section in *Chapter 11, Tooling and Troubleshooting* for more information on the cURL utility). To make the previous GET request, we simply issue the following command:

```
curl https://graph.facebook.com/v2.5/me/feed?limit=25&access_token=[ACCESS_TOKEN]
```

Doing so, you should get the following result:

![cURL command output in Windows cmd.exe showing feed data returned from graph.facebook.com]

Note that all of the feed data has been returned right in the terminal window for us to inspect immediately. cURL can also make POST requests, add headers, modify entity-body data, everything you need to test your OAuth 2.0 workflows! We will discuss this very useful tool in more depth in *Chapter 11, Tooling and Troubleshooting*.

Now we have two convenient ways for testing our API calls and access tokens (via the browser, and via cURL), both of which use the URI query parameter method for passing the access token. Knowing these two methods will help you greatly when debugging your application!

> **Only for testing!**
>
> It is worth mentioning again that this method for passing in your access token should only be used for testing purposes. If you utilize the URI query parameter method for passing your access token in your production applications, you will risk exposing your precious access tokens to unauthorized parties.

Send via the HTTP authorization header

We used the form-encoded body parameter method for our client-side example. For our server-side example, let's now use the authorization request header field. Making API calls by sending the access token via the HTTP authorization header is the most secure and preferred way of making API calls. As we mentioned earlier, all we have to do is add an authorization header and use as its value the token type followed by the token value. We can do this in our application using the Apache HTTP Client library with the following code:

```
import java.util.ArrayList;
import java.util.List;

import org.apache.http.NameValuePair;
import org.apache.http.client.entity.UrlEncodedFormEntity;
import org.apache.http.message.BasicNameValuePair;

...

// Request feed data with access token
String requestUrl =
  "https://graph.facebook.com/v2.5/me/feed?limit=25";
httpClient = HttpClients.createDefault();
httpPost = new HttpPost(requestUrl);
httpPost.addHeader("Authorization", "Bearer " + accessToken);
List<NameValuePair> urlParameters = new
  ArrayList<NameValuePair>();
urlParameters.add(new BasicNameValuePair("method", "get"));
httpPost.setEntity(new UrlEncodedFormEntity(urlParameters));
httpResponse = httpClient.execute(httpPost);

// Extract feed data from response
bufferedReader = new BufferedReader(
  new InputStreamReader(httpResponse.getEntity().getContent()));
String feedJson = bufferedReader.readLine();
System.out.println("Feed data: " + feedJson);
```

Notice that after we make the request, we extract the content from the response and print it to the console. If we have made our request correctly, our response should contain our feed data:

```
Mercury:wmiig charles$ sudo mvn -Dmaven.tomcat.port=80 -Dmaven.tomcat.path=/ tomcat:run
Password:
[INFO] Scanning for projects...
[INFO]
[INFO] ------------------------------------------------------------------------
[INFO] Building wmiig Maven Webapp 1.0-SNAPSHOT
[INFO] ------------------------------------------------------------------------
[INFO]
[INFO] >>> tomcat-maven-plugin:1.1:run (default-cli) > compile @ wmiig >>>
[INFO]
[INFO] --- maven-resources-plugin:2.6:resources (default-resources) @ wmiig ---
[WARNING] Using platform encoding (UTF-8 actually) to copy filtered resources, i.e. build is platform dependent!
[INFO] Copying 0 resource
[INFO]
[INFO] --- maven-compiler-plugin:3.1:compile (default-compile) @ wmiig ---
[INFO] Changes detected - recompiling the module!
[WARNING] File encoding has not been set, using platform encoding UTF-8, i.e. build is platform dependent!
[INFO] Compiling 1 source file to /Users/charles/wmiig/target/classes
[INFO]
[INFO] <<< tomcat-maven-plugin:1.1:run (default-cli) < compile @ wmiig <<<
[INFO]
[INFO] --- tomcat-maven-plugin:1.1:run (default-cli) @ wmiig ---
[INFO] Running war on http://localhost:80/
[INFO] Using existing Tomcat server configuration at /Users/charles/wmiig/target/tomcat
Nov 07, 2015 9:29:44 PM org.apache.catalina.startup.Embedded start
INFO: Starting tomcat server
Nov 07, 2015 9:29:45 PM org.apache.catalina.core.StandardEngine start
INFO: Starting Servlet Engine: Apache Tomcat/6.0.29
Nov 07, 2015 9:29:45 PM org.apache.coyote.http11.Http11Protocol init
INFO: Initializing Coyote HTTP/1.1 on http-80
Nov 07, 2015 9:29:45 PM org.apache.coyote.http11.Http11Protocol start
INFO: Starting Coyote HTTP/1.1 on http-80
Feed data: {"data":[{"id":"10101077671_10160214511","from":{"name":"John Se...
```

That's it! Plug this into your application and we have now fully implemented an OAuth 2.0 flow to, not only authenticate your user, but also make an API call to access that user's feed data!

> **Check your work on GitHub!**
>
> The full implementation for our server-side example application is available for viewing on our public GitHub account! See it at https://github.com/mastering-oauth-2/server-side-example.

Creating the world's most interesting infographic

We've now concluded our exploration of the various methods for passing our access token in an API call. We did this by demonstrating API calls to two of Facebook's APIs: one to fetch the profile data of the user, and the other to fetch the feed data of the user. You can now use this data in your application to generate all sorts of interesting statistics about your users. We will leave this as an exercise for you.

You can see an example of what can be accomplished with this data. Simply visit the following website:

`www.worldsmostinterestinginfographic.com`

This website is a production version of the server-side example that we've built in this book. Let this be a very simple example of what can be accomplished in a short amount of time using the OAuth 2.0 protocol to interface with a world-class service provider like Facebook!

> **See it on GitHub!**
>
> The full implementation for this entire web application is available for viewing on our public GitHub account too! See it at `https://github.com/mastering-oauth-2/worldsmostinterestinginfographic.com`. Let this be a simple example of what can be accomplished quite easily with OAuth 2.0!

Summary

In this chapter, we were finally able to complete the OAuth 2.0 workflow we've been learning about since the beginning of the book. We were able to utilize the access token we fetched in the previous two chapters to request access to a protected resource on the user's behalf. We examined three ways of doing this, each with their own pros and cons and appropriate scenarios for usage. We should now be able to integrate comfortably with the bulk of OAuth 2.0 service providers!

Chapter 7

Reference pages

Use these pages as reference documentation when requesting access to a protected resource in your application. Adapted from *The OAuth 2.0 Authorization Framework: Bearer Token Usage* specification [RFC 6750].

An overview of protected resource access

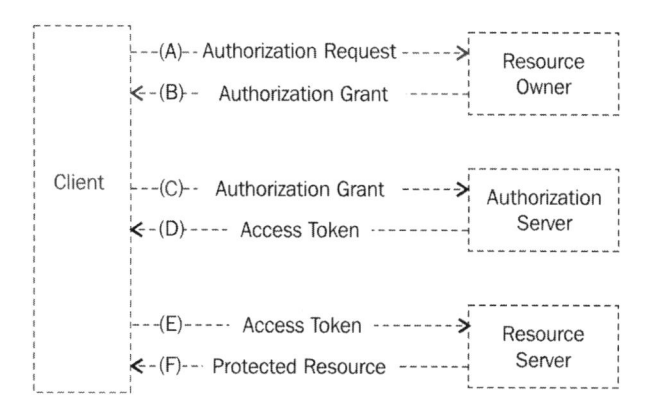

```
             +--(A)-- Authorization Request ----->  Resource
             <--(B)-- Authorization Grant  ------|  Owner

    Client   +--(C)-- Authorization Grant ----->  Authorization
             <--(D)---- Access Token ------------|  Server

             +--(E)----- Access Token ---------->  Resource
             <--(F)--- Protected Resource -------|  Server
```

Figure 1 from RFC 6750

The workflow for accessing a protected resource is described by steps (E) and (F), detailed as follows:

- **E**: The client requests the protected resource from the resource server and authenticates by presenting the access token.
- **F**: The resource server validates the access token, and if valid, serves the request.

[131]

The authorization request header field

When sending the access token in a protected resource access request using the authorization request header field method, an `Authorization` header must be added with its value set as the token type, which is `bearer`, followed by the token value.

An example of a protected resource access request using this method is:

```
GET /resource HTTP/1.1
Host: server.example.com
Authorization: Bearer mF_9.B5f-4.1JqM
```

This is the preferred method for passing your access token to the service provider. Use this whenever it is available.

The form-encoded body parameter

When sending the access token in a protected resource access request using the form-encoded body parameter method, you must pass it in as a URL-encoded parameter in a `POST` request.

An example of a protected resource access request using this method is:

```
POST /resource HTTP/1.1
Host: server.example.com
Content-Type: application/x-www-form-urlencoded

access_token=mF_9.B5f-4.1JqM
```

This can only be used if the following conditions have been met:

- The `Content-Type` header is included with its value set to `application/x-www-form-urlencoded`
- The entity-body contains only ASCII characters and is URL-encoded according to the `application/x-www-form-urlencoded` format
- The HTTP request body is single-part
- The HTTP request method has defined semantics for the request-body (that is, cannot use `GET`)

This method should only be used if the authorization request header field method is unavailable.

The URI query parameter

When sending the access token in a protected resource access request using the URI query parameter method, you must pass it in as a query parameter to the request URI.

An example of a protected resource access request using this method is:

```
GET /resource?access_token=mF_9.B5f-4.1JqM HTTP/1.1
Host: server.example.com
```

Clients using this method should also send a `Cache-Control` header containing the "no-store" option to prevent the caching of the access token in requests.

This method should only be used if both the authorization request header field method and the form-encoded body parameter method are unavailable.

8
Refresh Your Access Token

In the previous three chapters, we worked on the full end-to-end process of fetching an access token and using it to make an API call. We demonstrated this in a variety of ways, using the two most common methods for requesting an access token, as well as using the three methods for passing an access token in a protected resource access request. This works great for a single API call. However, what happens when you want to make multiple API calls over a longer period of time? Or, more specifically, how do we deal with expired access tokens? This is what we will be exploring next.

In this chapter, we will look at the optional workflow for refreshing your access token using what's called a **refresh token**. This workflow is described by the OAuth 2.0 specification, but is optional for service providers to support. So, in addition to looking at how to refresh your access token using a refresh token, we will also look at the alternative for refreshing your access token when your service provider doesn't support the refresh token workflow. Let's begin!

A closer look at the refresh token flow

If you recall from our discussion on access tokens in *Chapter 3*, *Four Easy Steps*, access tokens don't live forever. They have an expiry time which is often quite brief, usually on the order of minutes or hours. When your access token finally expires, what do you do? If your client is trusted, is using the authorization code grant flow, and the service provider you are integrating with supports the refresh token flow, then you can use a refresh token to fetch a new, valid access token.

To find out whether or not your service provider supports the refresh token flow, refer to their documentation. If so, you can expect to see a `refresh_token` value returned alongside your `access_token` value in your access token response (only with the authorization code grant flow). If you don't see this refresh token value present, then your service provider probably doesn't support it. However, if they do, you can make a refresh request, passing in this refresh token value, to gain a new, valid access token, all without user intervention. Let's look at this process now.

The refresh request

This is the request used by the client to ask the service provider for a new, valid access token. It is very similar to the access token request that you made in *Chapter 6, Get an Access Token with the Server-Side Flow*, with only a few small, but important, differences.

According to the specification

In order to request a new access token using the refresh token flow, we must make a `POST` request to the service provider's token endpoint, passing along a certain set of parameters, including the refresh token. The parameters must be encoded using the `application/x-www-form-urlencoded` format. In general terms, the template for the access token request is:

```
POST /token HTTP/1.1
Host: server.example.com
Authorization: Basic [ENCODED_CLIENT_CREDENTIALS]
Content-Type: application/x-www-form-urlencoded

grant_type=refresh_token&refresh_token=[REFRESH_TOKEN]
```

The parameters that can be added to the preceding request body are defined as:

- `grant_type`: (Required) Must be set to `refresh_token` to signify that we are requesting a new, valid access token, utilizing our refresh token.
- `refresh_token`: (Required) Our refresh token value.
- `scope`: (Optional) You may omit this from your request if you are requesting an access token with identical scope to the one you want to refresh. You may also request an access token with less scope than the one you wish to refresh. You may not, however, request an access token with a larger scope than was requested for the original access token. That is, your refreshed access token must contain an equal, or lesser, scope than the original access token.

In addition to passing in these parameters to the access token request, the client application must also identify itself with the service provider. Just as we did for the access token request in the server-side example application, we must pass an `Authorization` header with the header value being our client credentials encoded using the basic auth protocol. You'll notice that nearly everything about this refresh request is the same as our access token request in the authorization code grant flow, except for the parameters we pass in the request body.

> **Not in our application**
>
> Facebook, at the time of this writing, does not actually support the refresh token workflow. Because of this, we cannot implement this in our sample applications. This is a good example of a service provider that chooses not to implement such a feature. Instead, they provide alternative methods for long-lived sessions, such as long-lived access tokens and offline access support. Make sure you refer to your service provider's documentation to see how they handle long-lived sessions.

The access token response

If we constructed our refresh request correctly, and our refresh token is still valid, we can expect a new, valid access token to be returned to us. Otherwise, an error will be returned. This response structure, both success and error, is actually identical to the success and error responses to the access token request used in the authorization code grant flow. Although it is identical, we are including the documentation here again, for your convenience.

Success

If our refresh request was successful, the following parameters will be sent back in the entity-body of the response:

- `access_token`: (Required) This is what we're after! The presence of this value in the response is indicative of a successful refresh request.
- `token_type`: (Required) This defines the type of the token returned. This value is case-insensitive.
- `expires_in`: (Optional) The lifetime of the token in seconds. For example, if this value is 3600, that means that the access token will expire in one hour from the time the response message was generated. It is optional in that the service provider may not always return this value.

- `refresh_token`: (Optional) In response to a successful refresh request, a new refresh token may be issued back to you.
- `scope`: (Conditionally required) If the granted scope is identical to what was requested, this value may be omitted. However, if the granted scope is different from the requested scope, it must be present.

An example refresh token response for our application may look like:

```
HTTP/1.1 200 OK
Content-Type: application/json;charset=UTF-8
Cache-Control: no-store
Pragma: no-cache

{
  "access_token":"2YotnFZFEjr1zCsicMWpAA",
  "token_type":"bearer",
  "expires_in":3600,
  "refresh_token":"tGzv3JOkF0XG5Qx2TlKWIA"
}
```

Error

If your refresh request gets rejected for any reason, an access token will not be returned. Instead, the server will respond with an HTTP 400 (Bad Request) status code, including the following parameters in the body:

- `error`: (Required) This is a single code representing the error that caused the request to fail. The value must be one of the following:
    - `invalid_request`: The request is malformed and could not be processed
    - `invalid_client`: Client authentication failed
    - `invalid_grant`: The provided grant was invalid
    - `unauthorized_client`: The client application isn't authorized to make such a request
    - `unsupported_grant_type`: The authorization grant type is not supported
    - `invalid_scope`: The scope passed in is invalid

- **error_description**: (Optional) A human-readable message describing what caused the error.
- **error_uri**: (Optional) A link to a web document containing more information about the error.

An example response for our application would be:

```
HTTP/1.1 400 Bad Request
Content-Type: application/json;charset=UTF-8
Cache-Control: no-store
Pragma: no-cache

{
  "error":"invalid_client"
}
```

What if I have no refresh token? Or my refresh token has expired?

As we mentioned earlier, some service providers simply don't support the refresh token flow. Additionally, even if they do, refresh tokens also expire. Their lifetime is usually much longer, on the order of days or weeks—compared to minutes or hours with access tokens—but, nonetheless, they will expire eventually. So we must be prepared to handle the case where we want to get a new access token, but lack a valid refresh token to use to do so.

Our only alternative, in this case, would be to start the auth process again. To do this, we will essentially log the user back in as if we have never seen them before, starting the entire authorization request process, with whatever flow you like (implicit or authorization code grant) all over again.

For some service providers, this will force them to re-login, and possibly re-authorize your application. But, for many other service providers, they will resume the user's session and issue an access token immediately, without requiring the user's interaction. For such service providers, the user experience can be made to be nearly seamless, practically the same as if the refresh token flow were supported.

Comparison between the two methods

The following chart summarizes the differences between the two methods:

Method	Pros	Cons	Notes
Refresh token flow	• Can refresh the access token without user intervention, making for a seamless user experience • Minimizes the number of times the user sends their credentials across the Internet	• Optional, and so not supported by all OAuth 2.0 implementers and service providers	• If available, this method is preferred over the "starting over" method • Not supported when the client is untrusted (that is, using the implicit grant flow)
Starting auth process over again	• Simple design, essentially treating the user as if they are being seen for the first time	• Depending on how the service provider handles sessions, this may require user intervention to get a new access token (such as re-login, re-authorize, or both)	

The ideal workflow

When designing your application, you will want to utilize all of the tools and workflows at your disposal to achieve a user experience that is as seamless as possible. Now, given all of the information we have presented in this book thus far, we can create an optimal behavior workflow that our application can follow that makes the best use of the available workflows to minimize any user interactions that the user will have to do before your application can make API calls:

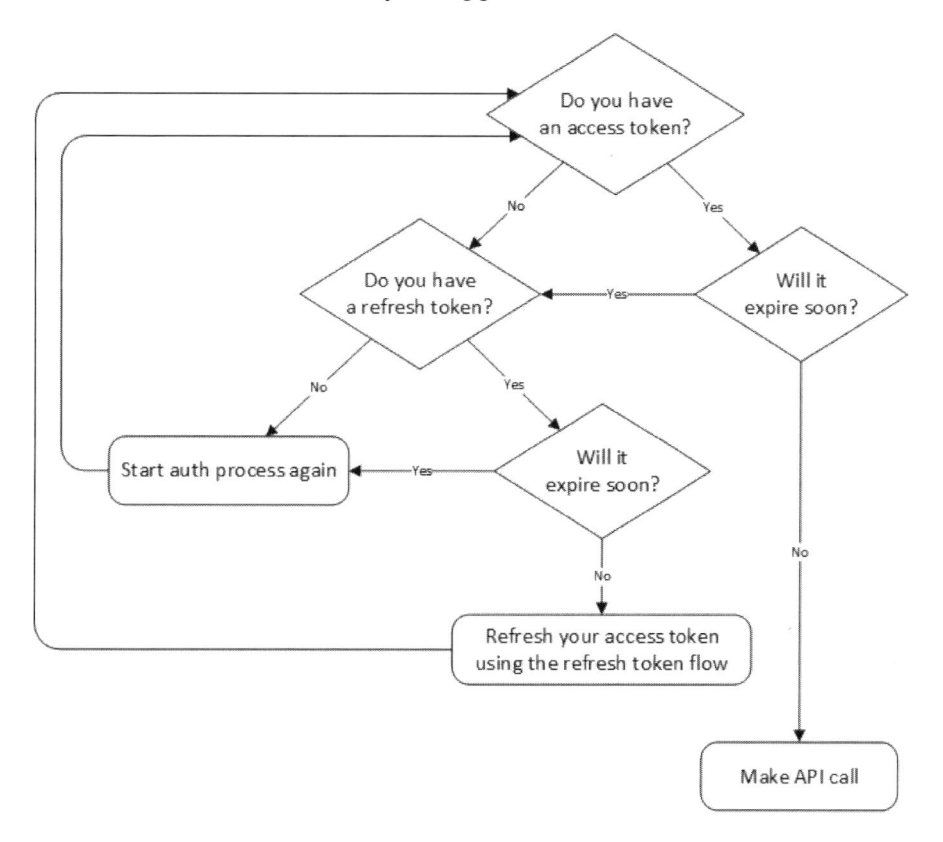

In the preceding flow diagram, we start with an access token. We continue to make API calls while the token is valid. Once the token becomes invalid (either because the API calls return with an `invalid_token` error, or we calculated the time of expiry in anticipation of its invalidation), we must fetch a new access token. If we have a refresh token, we can use that. If that refresh request fails because the refresh token has itself expired, or if we don't have a refresh token at all, then we must resort to starting the auth process all over again.

Utilizing a workflow like this in your application will maximize your use of your various tokens, using them for the duration of their lifetimes rather than requesting new ones when they aren't yet needed. It will also minimize the number of times your application will require user intervention.

Summary

In this chapter, we explored the various options for refreshing an access token. We looked at refreshing an access token using the preferred refresh token flow. We also looked at the always-available fallback plan of starting the entire auth process over again. Both of these achieve the same result (getting a new, valid access token), but with varying degrees of user interaction. Finally, we ended with a flow chart that models an ideal workflow for gaining and using access tokens, which minimizes user interaction.

This chapter concludes the part of the book in which we examine the different OAuth 2.0 flows and capabilities. In the next chapter, and continuing until the end of the book, we will be looking at the finer details of OAuth 2.0 to give you a more advanced understanding of the protocol and how to utilize it in the most effective and secure manner.

Chapter 8

Reference pages

Use these pages as reference documentation when implementing the implicit grant flow in your application. Adapted from *The OAuth 2.0 Authorization Framework* specification [RFC 6749].

An overview of the refresh token flow

```
          ------(A)--------- Authorization Grant --------->
                              Access Token
          <-----(B)---------------------------------------
                             & Refresh Token

          ------(C)---- Access Token --------->
                                                  Resource         Authorization
  Client  <-----(D)· Protected Resource-------    Server              Server
          ------(E)-- Access Token  --------->

          <-----(F)· Invalid Token Error -------

          ------(G)------------ Refresh Token -------------->
          <-----(H)----------- Access Token -----------------
                            & Optional Refresh Token
```

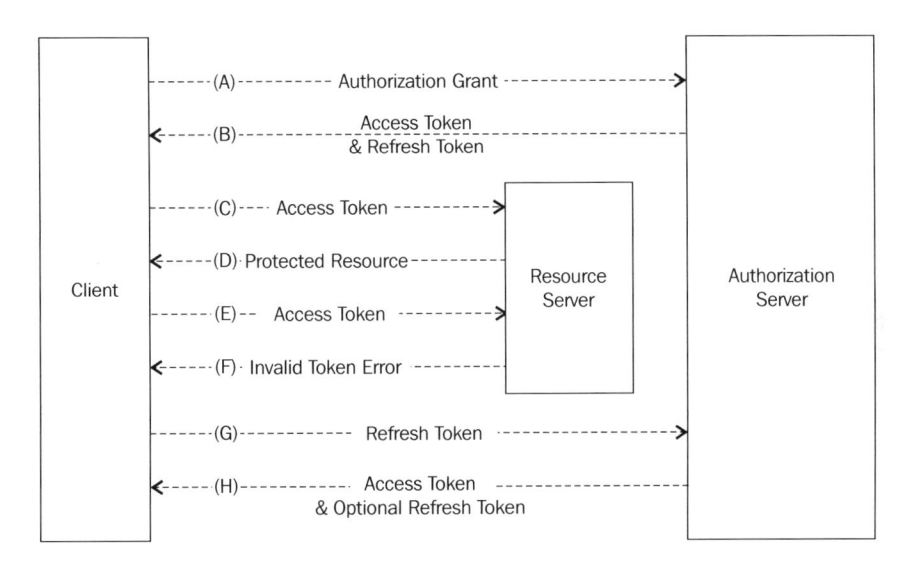

Figure 2 from RFC 6749

The steps are as follows:

- **A**: The client requests an access token by authenticating with the service provider and presenting an authorization grant.

- **B**: The authorization server of the service provider authenticates the client and validates the authorization grant and, if valid, issues an access token and optionally a refresh token.

- **C**: The client makes a protected resource request to the resource server by presenting the access token.

- **D**: The resource server validates the access token and, if valid, serves the request.

- **E**: Steps (**C**) and (**D**) repeat until the access token expires. If the client application knows the access token has expired, or will expire shortly, it may skip to step (**G**). Otherwise, the client application makes another protected resource request.

[143]

- **F**: Since the access token is invalid, the service provider returns an invalid token error.
- **G**: The client requests a new access token by authenticating with the service provider and presenting the refresh token.
- **H**: The authorization server authenticates the client, validates the refresh token, and, if valid, issues a new access token and, optionally, a new refresh token.

The refresh request

The client makes a POST request to the service provider's token endpoint, passing in the following parameters encoded using the `application/x-www-form-urlencoded` format as described in Appendix B of the specification:

- `grant_type`: (Required) Value must be set to `refresh_token`.
- `refresh_token`: (Required) The refresh token issued to the client.
- `scope`: (Optional) A list of space-delimited, case-sensitive strings which represent the scope of the access granted. The requested scope must not include any scope not originally granted by the user and, if omitted, is treated as equal to the scope originally granted by the resource owner.

An example refresh request looks like:

```
POST /token HTTP/1.1
Host: server.example.com
Authorization: Basic czZCaGRSa3F0MzpnWDFmQmF0M2JW
Content-Type: application/x-www-form-urlencoded

grant_type=refresh_token&
  refresh_token=tGzv3JOkF0XG5Qx2TlKWIA
```

Access token response

If the refresh request is valid and authorized, the response will contain an access token, optional refresh token, and other parameters described as follows:

- `access_token`: (Required) The access token issued by the service provider.
- `token_type`: (Required) The type of the token issued. This value is case-insensitive.

- `expires_in`: (Optional) The lifetime of the access token given in seconds. If omitted, the service provider should communicate the expiration time via other means.
- `refresh_token`: (Optional) A refresh token, which can be used to obtain new access tokens using the refresh token workflow.
- `scope`: (Conditionally required) A list of space-delimited, case-sensitive strings which represent the scope of the access granted. Required only if the scope granted is different from the scope requested.

An example access token response looks like:

```
HTTP/1.1 200 OK
Content-Type: application/json;charset=UTF-8
Cache-Control: no-store
Pragma: no-cache

{
  "access_token":"2YotnFZFEjr1zCsicMWpAA",
  "token_type":"bearer",
  "expires_in":3600,
  "refresh_token":"tGzv3JOkF0XG5Qx2TlKWIA",
  "example_parameter":"example_value"
}
```

Error response

If the refresh request fails for any reason, the server will respond with an HTTP 400 (Bad Request) status code including the following properties:

- `error`: (Required) This is a single error code representing the condition that caused the request to fail. The value must be one of the following:
    - `invalid_request`: The request is missing a required parameter, includes an unsupported parameter value (other than grant type), repeats a parameter, includes multiple credentials, utilizes more than one mechanism for authenticating the client, or is otherwise malformed
    - `invalid_client`: Client authentication failed for some reason (for example, unknown client, no client authentication included, or unsupported authentication method)
    - `invalid_grant`: The provided authorization grant or refresh token is invalid, expired, revoked, does not match the redirection URI used in the authorization request, or was issued to another client

- - unauthorized_client: The authenticated client is not authorized to use this authorization grant type
  - unsupported_grant_type: The authorization grant type is not supported by the authorization server
  - invalid_scope: The requested scope is invalid, unknown, malformed, or exceeds the scope granted by the user
- error_description: (Optional) A human-readable ASCII message providing additional information regarding the error.
- error_uri: (Optional) A URI identifying a human-readable web page that provides additional information regarding the error.

An example error response looks like:

```
HTTP/1.1 400 Bad Request
Content-Type: application/json;charset=UTF-8
Cache-Control: no-store
Pragma: no-cache

{
  "error":"invalid_request"
}
```

9
Security Considerations

Up until this point in the book, we have examined the OAuth 2.0 protocol in depth. We have looked at why it is important, where it is used, and how it operates. We have then used this knowledge to implement our own OAuth 2.0 client that interacts with Facebook.

In this chapter, we cover a very important topic: security. We will discuss some security best practices as well as look at some common attacks that you will want to be aware of when creating your own client application. But, before we do, in order to get an accurate idea of the importance of a secure client application that utilizes OAuth 2.0, let's discuss what is at stake.

What's at stake?

Just as with any application, security should be a top priority. This is especially true for applications that utilize the OAuth 2.0 protocol. In order to understand why this is true, let's remember what OAuth 2.0 actually does for us. Recall that, in the first chapter, we discussed how OAuth 2.0 provides us with federated identity as well as delegated authority. If we aren't diligent with our security practices during implementation, we can expose some very dangerous holes for attackers to exploit. And, when dealing with federated identity and delegated authority, we must be extra vigilant since these are very powerful practices that can provide attackers with a lot of power.

If an attacker were somehow able to exploit your application to game either of these concepts, they may be able to do the following:

- Impersonate users
- Impersonate client applications
- Grant themselves otherwise unauthorized permissions
- Gain access to protected data and resources

In order to combat this, we must be extra careful with our implementation with regard to the client integration with the service provider via OAuth 2.0. Let's start by looking at some best practices that you can implement in your own application.

Security best practices

Security is a never-ending battle. There are countless ways that a given application can be exploited. As engineers, our job is to minimize the attack vectors available to attackers. We can never cover all of the holes, but it is still our duty to try. What follows is a non-exhaustive list of security best practices that will help to keep your application as secure as possible.

Use TLS!

This may seem like an obvious tip, but it is important enough to note. *Use secure communication channels!* This applies for when your client application talks to service providers, as well as when the service providers talk to your client application.

When your client application talks to the service provider, it does so by interacting with their authorization and token endpoints. You must ensure that they utilize TLS so that your communication with them is secure and encrypted.

> **Make sure the service provider uses TLS**
> Verify that the authorization and token endpoints that your client application uses to talk to the service provider both start with `https`.

Additionally, when the service provider talks back to your client application, it does so via the redirect URI that you pass to it. You must make sure that this endpoint, which you own, utilizes TLS as well.

> **Make sure your client application uses TLS**
> Verify that the redirect URI that you pass to the service provider in requests starts with `https`.

> **The OAuth 2.0 Authorization Framework**
>
> The OAuth 2.0 specification actually mandates the use of TLS by the service provider. That is, the authorization and token endpoints that your client application will be interacting with should already use TLS.
>
> However, the use of TLS by the client application is optional. This decision was made to reduce the number of barriers for developers to create OAuth 2.0-compliant client applications due to the added complexity required for client developers to implement (purchase and install SSL certificates). It was a usability decision and not a security decision.
>
> Because of this, many application developers will operate without TLS during some portion of development. But when approaching production, you should switch to using TLS.

Request minimal scopes

Recall that a scope is simply a permission that your client application is requesting on behalf of the user. Make sure that you are requesting only what is needed by your application, and no more. This may seem obvious, but as applications grow and evolve, their functionality changes with it. This may change the scope of the permissions that your application requires.

> **Keep track of what your application needs**
>
> Regularly audit your requested scopes to make sure they are the minimal set required for your application to function. This may change over time.

When using the implicit grant flow, request read-only permissions

Recall, clients that utilize the implicit grant flow are untrusted clients. They are considered untrusted because they do not have a backend server to facilitate secure communication with the service provider. So, when the service provider sends tokens to the client, it does so by attaching the token values to the URL fragment of the redirect URI. Because of this, those token values are available to the user and anyone else who has access to the user-agent. Additionally, the value may be cached in some access logs or browser history for an attacker to find.

Tokens granted to untrusted clients are inherently insecure for these reasons. Keeping this in mind, you should only request read-only permissions when utilizing the implicit grant flow from untrusted clients. This minimizes the risk in the case that a token gets leaked.

> **Assume tokens granted to untrusted clients are available to everyone**
>
> Request read-only permissions from clients using the implicit grant flow to minimize the risk associated with leaked tokens.

Keep credentials and tokens out of reach of users

Your application's client credentials and the received tokens are sensitive properties. You must keep these as secure as possible, making sure not to expose them to users. It is assumed that, if a user can see them, an attacker can too. If an attacker can get hold of your application's client credentials, they can impersonate your client. If an attacker can get hold of a granted access token for a user, they can impersonate that user. It is best to keep these out of reach of the users entirely. This is best done by using a backend server to store and transmit these values, never exposing them to the client.

> **If a user can see it, so can an attacker**
>
> Store your client credentials and tokens on a backend server that is not available to users. Communicate with the service provider from this backend server as well. This further keeps those sensitive properties out of the reach of clients, and attackers.

This leads well into our next point.

Use the authorization code grant flow whenever possible

The authorization code grant flow is the most secure flow available for OAuth 2.0 integration. It utilizes a backend server to securely store and transmit sensitive properties, such as client credentials and tokens, to and from the service provider. Proper use of a server to facilitate these communications will completely abstract, and hide, the flows from the end-user, as well as any attackers.

> **The authorization code grant flow is the most secure**
>
> Because of the presence of a backend server for clients that use the authorization code grant flow, these clients can make secure communications to the service provider that aren't visible to users and attackers, making this the most secure, and preferred, grant flow to use.

If you cannot use a backend server for some reason, or choose not to for certain use cases, refer to the previous *When using the implicit grant flow, request read-only permissions* section.

Use the refresh token whenever possible

For clients using the authorization code grant flow, depending on the service provider, a refresh token may be returned to the client. When an access token expires for a user, rather than requiring them to authenticate again, the refresh token can be used to request a new, valid access token. This is desirable from both a security standpoint as well as a usability standpoint. In terms of security, the fewer times a user has to authenticate means the fewer times a user has to send their username and password across the Internet. This also means fewer opportunities for an attacker to steal them. From a usability standpoint, this means that your application can function for longer periods of time without having to ask your users to re-log in.

> **Refresh tokens reduce the number of times your users have to re-authenticate**
>
> Making effective use of refresh tokens can minimize the opportunities attackers have to steal user credentials, as well as provide a better user experience by extending their sessions with your client without intervention.

Use native browsers instead of embedded browsers

The use of native external browsers over embedded browsers pertains particularly to native applications (that is, desktop applications and mobile applications). Often, when implementing a native application, you can choose to initiate the authorization flow in either the native system browser or an embedded browser within your application.

Security Considerations

For example, if you are developing an iPhone application and want to start the authorization flow for a user, you can choose to do this through the native iPhone Safari browser. Or, you can choose to use an embedded browser provided by the SDK directly in your application. This choice has many important, but subtle, consequences, relating to both security and usability.

Initially, you may want to use an embedded browser for your application. This will provide a more seamless user experience since users can stay in your application without having to bring the native system browser to the front momentarily for authentication and authorization. However, there are some very good reasons to use the native system browser.

The most important reason for using the native system browser is that you can leverage the system chrome to display security information related to the target service provider's authorization endpoint. For instance, native browsers will often display warnings for sites with invalid or expired certificates, whereas embedded browsers often do not. This makes phishing attacks easier. (Refer to *Phishing* in the *Common attacks* section later in this chapter for more information.)

Native system browsers use a different cookie jar than embedded browsers. So, if a user already has an active session in the system browser, they can piggyback on this. Whereas, in an embedded browser, since sessions aren't shared with the native browser, they will likely have to start a new session.

Additionally, native system browsers may have plugins available to it, like password managers, which would not be available to embedded browsers.

The following chart displays a short summary of the pros and cons of native browsers versus embedded browsers:

Native external system browser	Embedded browser
Pros: • Makes use of system chrome which can display important security information related to the currently loaded page. • Uses the system cookie store, so it is able to take advantage of already-active sessions. • Plugins are available (for example, password managers).	Pros: • Provides a more seamless user experience since the user can stay within the context of the client application without having to switch contexts to a system browser to log in.

Native external system browser	Embedded browser
Cons: - A less than ideal user experience since it requires the system browser to be brought to the forefront for the user to authenticate and authorize.	Cons: - Does not often display the security information related to the currently loaded page. Makes phishing attacks easy since it is hard for users to confirm the validity of the page they are looking at. - Uses a different cookie store from the system browser. Users will most likely have to log in since they won't have a valid session with this browser. - No plugins available.

Do not use third-party scripts in the redirection endpoint

When constructing your redirection endpoint, make sure that you do not include any third-party or externally loaded scripts. These scripts have access to your redirection URI and the credentials it contains. It is possible that these scripts can be compromised and, if loaded externally, could leak your access tokens or authorization codes to attackers.

If you do choose to use third-party scripts, you must ensure that your scripts execute first to both extract and remove the credentials from the URI before allowing any other scripts to execute.

Ideally, your redirection endpoint will contain logic only to extract and remove the credentials before redirecting the user-agent to another page, all without exposing the credentials.

> **Third-party scripts should be untrusted**
> Your redirection endpoint should extract and remove any sensitive credentials before allowing other scripts to execute.

Security Considerations

> **How did we do?**
> You may notice that, in the sample code for our client-side example, we did not follow this best practice. We load the jQuery library at our redirection endpoint and use it to make our API call. We did this on purpose for the sake of clarity in our example code. However, if http://code.jquery.com/ (the site that hosts the library) ever got compromised, it is possible that an attacker can replace the library with a malicious version and poison our application and steal our tokens.

Rotate your client credentials

Just as you should for your own personal password, you should rotate your client credentials. This minimizes the attack vectors available to attackers since, if you rotate your credentials regularly, they will have a more limited time to utilize them if they are leaked.

A good practice would be to rotate these credentials with every release (or major release, depending on your security requirements and development cycle).

Common attacks

Now that we've looked at some security best practices to keep your application secure, let's now take a look at some common attacks against OAuth 2.0 clients that you should be aware of. We will also examine the mitigation techniques you can use to protect your application from such attacks.

Cross-site request forgery (CSRF)

Cross-site request forgery is a powerful attack that has been gaining popularity with attackers in recent years. It involves tricking users into following a malicious link that performs an undesirable action on a trusted site without their knowledge, making use of their pre-existing sessions with that site.

For instance, imagine a user has just logged into their bank in their favorite web browser. Now, in another tab, they open an e-mail from a malicious user with a link that says "See cats here!" which leads to http://www.catloversheaven.com/.

This site is owned by the attacker and, while the user is browsing cute cat pictures, in the background, the website silently makes a call to https://www.bank.com/transfer?to=37325283&amount=1000.

Since the user already has a valid session with their bank, this request will be seen as valid. And so, while the user is enjoying the attacker-owned cat website, they have also unwittingly transferred $1,000 out of their account and into the attacker's account.

This can be done in many ways: a malicious link that they trick victims into clicking, an iframe or image that automatically loads the malicious link, or even a redirection from an attacker-controlled page.

Now that we understand what CSRF is at a high-level, let's look at how it is relevant to an OAuth 2.0 client application. The following illustration demonstrates a typical authorization workflow between a client application and a service provider in two ways: first, in the normal fashion, and second, with a CSRF attack on the redirect URI for the client application.

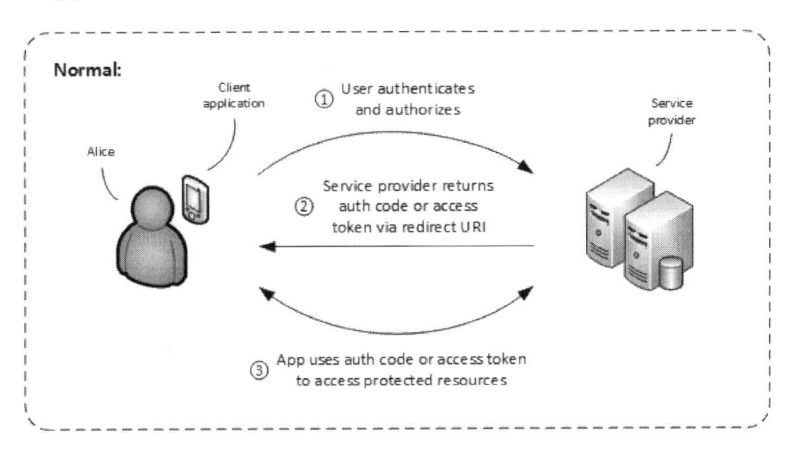

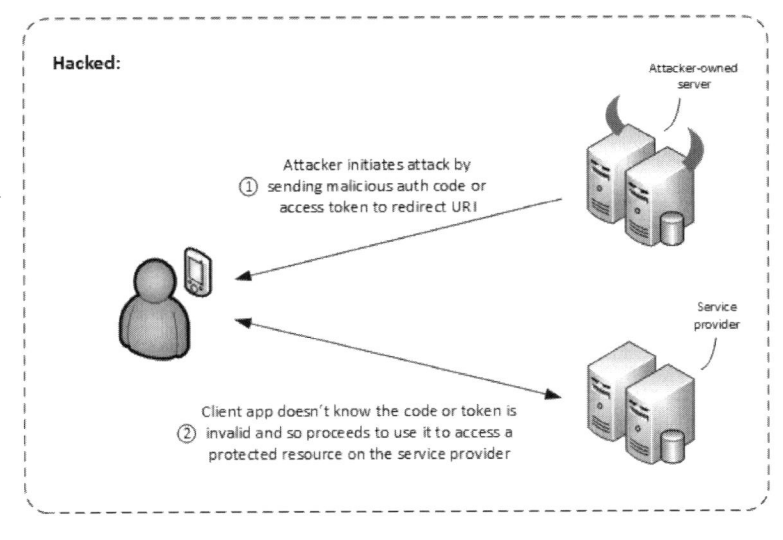

What's going on?

Note that the first workflow is the typical authorization workflow that we are used to. However, in the second workflow, we can see that there is another party, namely, the attacker. In this scenario, the attacker sends a malicious authorization code or access token directly to the client application's redirect URI. Since the client application can't verify that the token is valid, it continues to use it to communicate with the service provider. As the token is attacker-owned, this may result in the attacker gaining access to the protected resources of the user.

This happens mainly because the client application has no way of verifying that the authorization code or access token that has been issued to it is the result of a valid request made by the application. To combat this, the client application must make use of the `state` param.

Use the state param to combat CSRF

In order for your client application to protect against CSRF, your client application must gain the ability to verify whether the authorization codes or access tokens issued to it are valid (that is, they are the result of a valid authorization request by the user from your client application). To do this, your client application must generate a session-specific, unguessable value that it can pass along with its authorization request. When an authorization code or access token is returned back to the redirect URI, your application can validate that value to ensure that it was indeed used as part of a valid authorization request initiated by the user, and not by some attacker.

The following diagram demonstrates this process in action, showing both a successful and valid authorization flow, followed by an invalid, attacker-initiated flow:

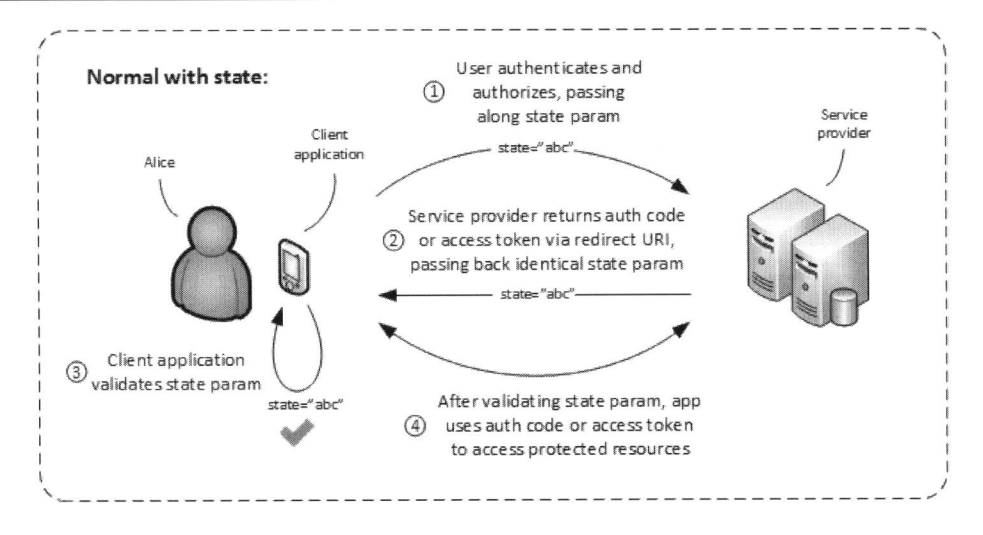

Normal with state:

① User authenticates and authorizes, passing along state param — state="abc"

② Service provider returns auth code or access token via redirect URI, passing back identical state param — state="abc"

③ Client application validates state param — state="abc"

④ After validating state param, app uses auth code or access token to access protected resources

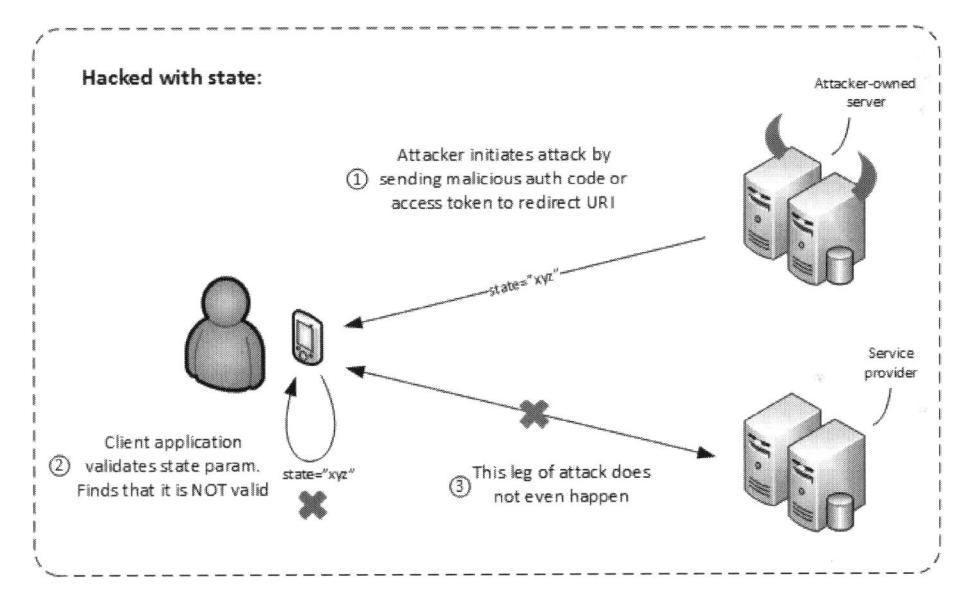

Hacked with state:

① Attacker initiates attack by sending malicious auth code or access token to redirect URI — state="xyz"

② Client application validates state param. Finds that it is NOT valid — state="xyz"

③ This leg of attack does not even happen

In the valid scenario, we can see that it is mostly the same as before. However, notice that with the authorization request, the client is passing along that unique, session-based, un-guessable `state` param value. In step 2, the user authenticates and the service provider will return an authorization code or access token back to the client application via the redirect URI, along with the `state` param value that was passed in with the initial request.

> If a `state` param value is passed to a service provider, the OAuth 2.0 specification mandates that it be returned back to the client application untouched. This mechanism is designed specifically to mitigate such CSRF attacks, and should be used particularly for this reason.

There is an added step, step 3, where the client application takes the returned `state` param and verifies that it is in fact a valid one. That is, it verifies that it was generated by the client application and used in a valid authorization request initiated by the user. If, and only if, this is true, will the application continue to interact with the service provider with the given tokens.

Notice in the second workflow, the attacker does not know this `state` param value since it is session-based and un-guessable. And so, when the attacker sends a malicious authorization code or access token to the client application's redirect URI, they will be unable to send along a valid `state` param. When the client application receives this malicious token, it sees that it has an invalid `state` param value, or none at all, and it halts the process right there. By simply generating and passing along a `state` param value, and validating it at the redirect endpoint, we have mitigated any CSRF attacks against the redirect endpoint.

Phishing

Phishing is an attack in which an attacker creates a page or application that looks similar or identical to a target site with the intention that users will be unaware that it is a duplicate and so will enter secret information, say a username and password, only to be captured by the impostor site.

OAuth 2.0 client applications are vulnerable to phishing because they rely on sending a user's user-agent to and from the service provider endpoints in order to delegate authority. When developing your client application, you should consider the security implications of how your users will interact with the service provider to authenticate. A good rule of thumb is to follow the best practice mentioned earlier in the *Use native browsers instead of embedded browsers* section.

If you use native external browsers in your application, your users will have an increased ability to verify the authenticity of the authorization endpoint that they are seeing.

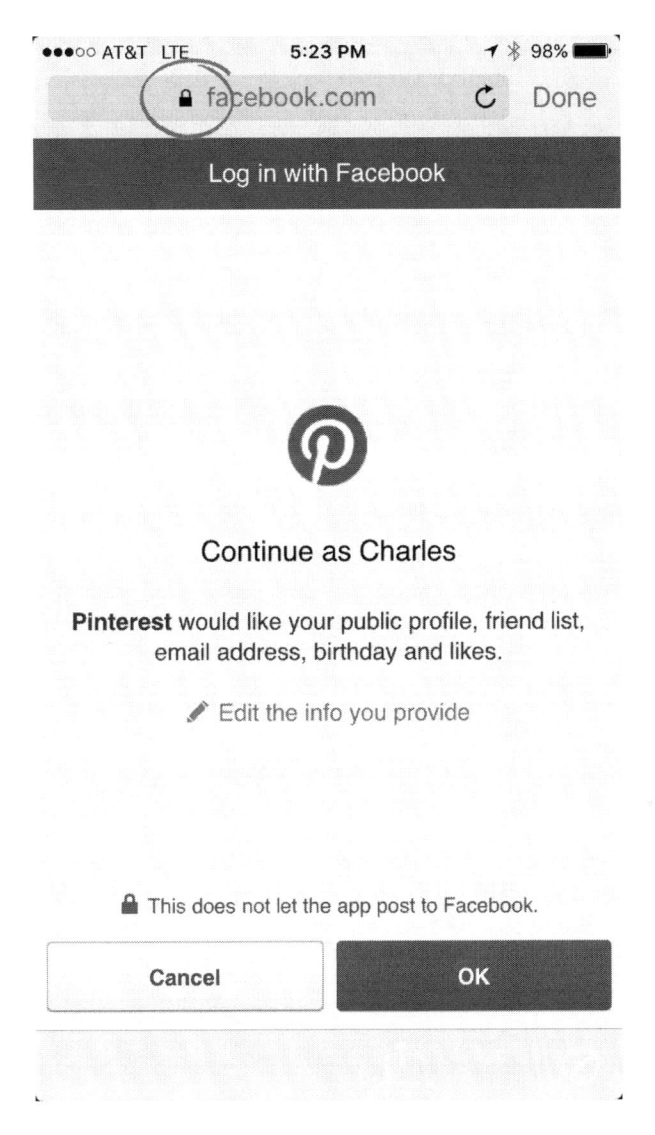

With native browsers, there are often more indicators of a site's validity (for example the lock next to the URL in iPhone's mobile Safari). This isn't the case with embedded browsers, which makes utilizing counterfeit pages much easier for attackers.

Redirection URI manipulation

When your client application makes an authorization request for a user, it passes along a `redirect_uri` parameter. If an attacker can manipulate the value of this redirection URI, they may be able to cause the service provider to redirect the user's user-agent to an endpoint that they control, along with the authorization code.

Furthermore, if your application allows users to own or create a webspace of some sort that they control, say a homepage or a user profile page, they may be able to leverage this as part of their attack.

For example, consider the scenario where the application GoodApp allows users to create a homepage on their domain. The user Eve may have a homepage that she controls at `www.goodapp.com/users/eve`. If the service provider that you are interacting with allows you to register wildcard redirect URIs, like `www.goodapp.com/*`, or doesn't require you to register your redirect URIs at all, then an attacker, such as Eve, would be able to use this homepage to her advantage.

What Eve could do is set up a fake link to log into your application, or even a counterfeit application entirely. When a user clicks on this link, they will be directed to the authorization endpoint of the service provider just as would be done from the real application. However, instead of passing the proper redirect URI, say `www.goodapp.com/callback`, this link passes her own malicious redirect URI which just happens to be her profile page, `www.goodapp.com/users/eve`. On this page, she can then intercept any authorization codes and access tokens, and proceed to impersonate your users and access their protected resources.

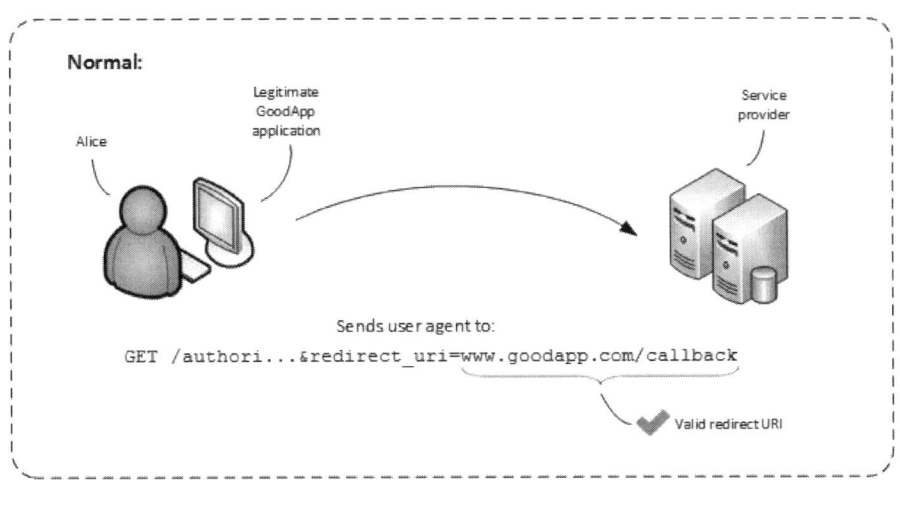

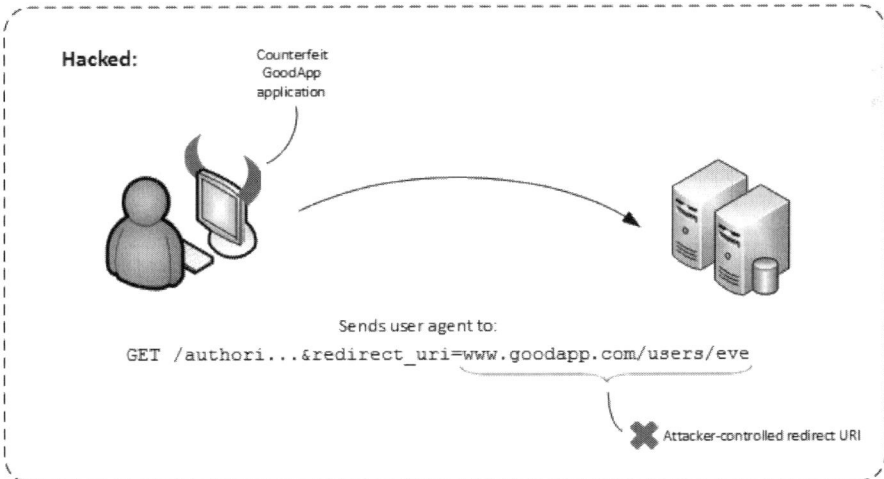

Notice in the preceding image that all Eve needs to do is convince a user to follow her malicious authorization link containing her attacker-controlled redirect URI. From the user's perspective, the user experience would be mostly the same since all that is different is the redirect URI (the attacker may choose to request additional scopes too!).

Security Considerations

To mitigate this, make sure that you register your redirect URIs. If the service provider that you are interacting with allows you to register wildcard redirect URIs, use them sparingly. You should always prefer to register fully-qualified redirect URIs over wildcard redirection endpoints. This is especially true if your service or application allows users to create a webspace that they control, say a homepage or profile page.

Client and user impersonation

A very basic attack that is often done is simple client or user impersonation. In client impersonation, an attacker masquerades as your client application in order to gain access to the user's protected resources. This can be achieved quite simply if an attacker is able to get access to your client credentials (that is, your client ID and client secret). With this, they would be able to impersonate your client to the service provider and to end users.

In user impersonation, an attacker will masquerade as the end user. This can be done if an attacker is able to gain access to an issued access token. With this, they would be able to make requests to the service provider to access protected resources on behalf of the user, just as your application does (recall what `bearer` in bearer token means from *Chapter 2, A Bird's Eye View of OAuth 2.0*).

To mitigate both of these attacks, the solution is simple: protect your client credentials, codes, and tokens from end users! If an attacker were able to see any of those, they would be granted the ability to impersonate your client application or your users, or both.

Summary

In this chapter, we discussed a lot of important topics relating to the security of your application. We looked at several best practices that should be observed when developing your application. It is important to be aware of all of these attack vectors, and mitigate any opportunities that you can for attackers to infiltrate your application. The best practices listed are good rules to follow, but they are not exhaustive. You should try and implement them all in your application. If you don't, at least have the understanding of the scenario so that you are prepared to deal with any attacks that may follow. We also looked at some of the most common attack scenarios on OAuth 2.0 clients, including methods to mitigate them. There are no silver bullets when it comes to security. All that we can do is try our best to plug any holes, and be vigilant in this effort as our application grows and evolves. In the next chapter, we will take a dedicated look at mobile applications and how they differ from traditional applications.

10
What About Mobile?

Application developers have a multitude of platforms to target and develop for. Traditionally, the platforms to develop for were the desktop platforms, be it Windows, Mac, or Linux/Unix. However, more recently, nothing has been growing faster than the mobile platforms: iPhone, Android, and Windows Mobile. Mobile platforms have become the largest platforms for the consumption of digital media today, overtaking desktops in recent years, and still growing! Because of this, we have dedicated an entire chapter to considerations for mobile application developers. Here, we will discuss special details particular to developing applications for mobile platforms. But first, let's take a step back and define what we consider a mobile application to be in the first place.

What is a mobile application?

The term "mobile application" is used quite loosely these days. Typically, when someone says "mobile application" they are referring to one of two types of applications:

- Mobile-optimized web application
- Natively installed mobile application

The first type is simply a web application that runs in the browser, but is optimized for the smaller screens typical in mobile devices like phones and tablets. This type of application is no different from any other web application. It executes in the browser, and so the same rules and considerations apply to it regardless of whether it is a mobile browser or a desktop browser.

The second, however, is of more importance to us. This type of application represents natively installed applications on mobile devices, an entirely new platform in recent years. From here on, when we mention "mobile applications", we are referring to this second category of applications, natively installed mobile applications, and not mobile-optimized web applications.

What flow should we use for mobile applications?

Just as developing any other type of client application, the type of flow to use should be decided based on the capabilities of the platform. However, mobile platforms are quite new and rich, and so added attention is required when making this decision. The two main flows are still available to us—implicit grant and authorization code grant. Recall that the implicit grant is designed for use in untrusted clients, while the authorization code grant is designed for use with trusted clients. Further recall that trusted clients are clients that are able to securely store and transmit their confidential properties. So, the question then becomes, are mobile applications considered trusted, or untrusted?

Are mobile applications trusted or untrusted?

In order for a mobile application to be considered trusted, it must be able to securely store and transmit confidential information. This can really only be achieved in one way, with the use of a backend server. If a mobile application has a backend server that powers it, this server can also be used to securely store and transmit any confidential information it needs to. In this case, yes, this particular type of mobile application can be considered trusted, and should therefore use the authorization code grant flow.

This is no different from desktop and web applications that are powered by a backend server. The presence and correct use of this backend server prevents users, and attackers alike, from gaining access to any confidential properties vital to your application. In the absence of this backend server though, your application will be unable to securely store and transmit confidential information, and cannot be considered trusted. In this case, your mobile application should use the implicit grant flow.

What about mobile applications built on top of mobile platforms with secure storage APIs?

Not all mobile applications are powered by a backend server. Some mobile applications are standalone installations that interact with a service provider directly. For such applications, developers must leverage secure storage APIs (APIs designed for application developers to store application data securely on the device) supported by the mobile platform they are developing on. Most of the major mobile platforms today offer such secure storage APIs, each with their own unique names and usages, but all achieving the same thing. Here is a quick summary of some of the available secure storage APIs available for the three major mobile platforms at the time of this writing:

Platform	Secure storage APIs
iOS	Data protection
Android	Android keystore system
Windows Phone	DPAPI (Data Protection API)

If you are developing an application on one of these platforms, you can make use of these APIs to securely store your secrets. For the most part, this is enough for most applications to be considered trusted. You can store your client credentials here and communicate directly with the service provider through your application, accessing these secrets via the APIs without the use of a backend server.

Not quite enough

Strictly speaking, though, such an application that makes use of secure storage APIs to securely store their confidential properties is **not** considered trusted. It is much more secure than a typical web browser application, since web browsers don't have very reliable methods for securely storing confidential information. However, in strict terms, it is still not enough to be considered fully trusted. In order to understand why, let's look back at mobile applications that use a backend server.

The following is a diagram of a typical mobile application that uses a backend server for securely storing and transmitting confidential data:

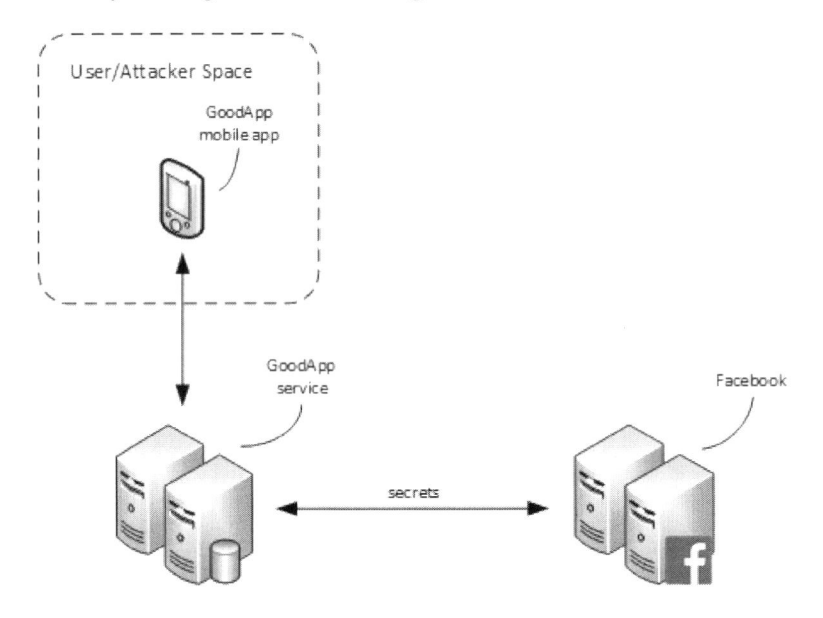

Notice how the application's secrets are stored and transmitted outside of the available space of the user and any attackers. In particular, attackers are unable to see the secret data in any form, encrypted or not encrypted, stored or in transit. In this model, it is impossible for an attacker to gain access to the secret data. This is a truly secure model and trusted client, fit for the authorization code grant flow.

Now, let's look at this same diagram, but this time with a mobile application that uses secure storage APIs of the platform it is on:

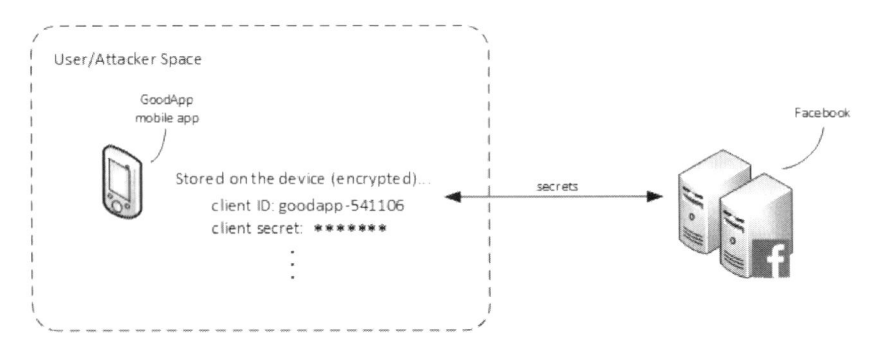

Notice, now, in this picture, all of the confidential data is stored on the device itself. It uses the secure storage APIs of the platform, and so it is stored encrypted somewhere on the device, but on the device nonetheless. Further, it is transmitted through the user/attacker space to the service provider. Presumably, it is transmitted via secure channels, but still, transmitted through the user/attacker space nonetheless.

In this model, the application developer is heavily relying on the security of the platform's secure storage APIs as well as the security of the transport protocol used. Now, these may well be extremely secure and difficult for attackers to break. But, in strict terms, it is possible. And, in the world of security, "possible" should be assumed probable, even certain. This is why mobile applications that don't have backend servers but make use of the mobile platform's secure storage APIs should **not** be considered trusted and should therefore not use the authorization code grant flow.

> **Maybe good enough after all**
>
> The preceding scenario paints a worst-case picture of security in relation to your application. In practical terms, it is likely sufficient for your application to make use of these secure storage APIs and be fine. However, if your application deals with extremely sensitive material, you will want to err on the side of caution and make sure to create a truly trusted application by making use of a backend server to facilitate secure storage and transmission of your confidential data.

Hybrid architectures

Mobile applications come in many shapes and sizes. As such, the architecture of your mobile application can be flexible as well. There is no reason why your application has to use a single authorization workflow, as is described in the preceding section. If you have a mobile application, and a backend server, you can create a hybrid architecture to leverage the best of both worlds.

Implicit for mobile app, authorization code grant for backend server

Most service providers support the idea of having a single client use multiple authorization flows. For example, Facebook supports a single client application using both the implicit grant flow and the authorization code grant flow. We can leverage this capability and use the most appropriate flow for the given task. For instance, if your application requires some non-sensitive data in a read-only manner, this can be made directly from your native mobile application via the implicit grant flow. Your application may also require some more sensitive data, or may need to write some data or make changes to a property with the service provider. In this case, it is appropriate to make this call from the server using the authorization code grant flow. The following diagram illustrates a simple example of such a hybrid architecture:

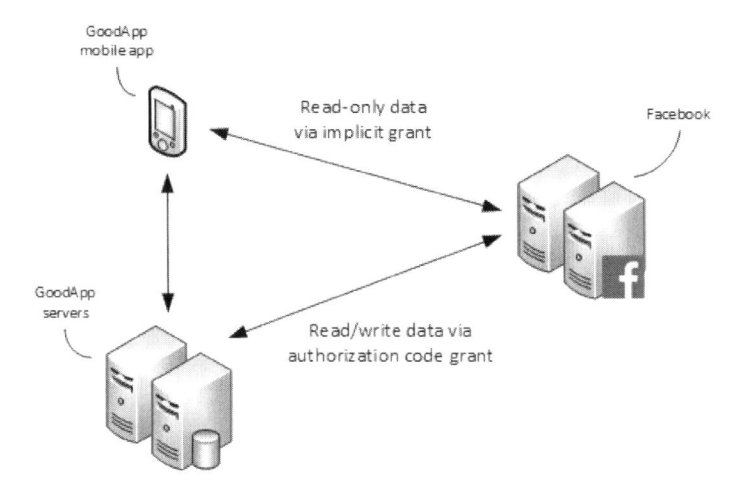

With the preceding architecture, the mobile application can request directly to the service provider using the implicit grant flow. You must remember to follow the best practices from the previous chapter regarding the use of the implicit grant flow in the *When using the implicit grant flow, request read-only permissions* section.

When your application needs to perform more complex tasks, greater than simply fetching read-only, insensitive data, you will want to do this from the server using the authorization code grant flow. This allows you to still allow your application to perform powerful tasks, while still keeping the confidentiality of your secrets.

What is the benefit of this?

Using a hybrid architecture, like the one described in the preceding section, allows your application to optimize simple workflows from the mobile application, while still allowing your application to perform complex, powerful tasks with the use of the server. You are also able to maximize the performance of your application while still maintaining a high level of security.

Authorization via application instead of user-agent

With the typical OAuth 2.0 authorization flow, your application will direct your user's user-agent to the service provider's authorization endpoint where they can log in and authorize your application. However, in the world of mobile applications, certain platforms and service providers support the ability to perform this authorization flow within the service provider's mobile application and not with a user-agent.

What About Mobile?

For example, if you were to write a mobile application that integrates with Facebook, typically, when your user goes to authenticate, your application will send their user-agent to Facebook's authorization endpoint. However, Facebook on iOS allows this operation to happen via the Facebook application itself. That is, instead of sending the user's user-agent to Facebook in mobile Safari for them to log in and authorize your application, your application can instead open up Facebook's iPhone application and let the user perform the authorization from there:

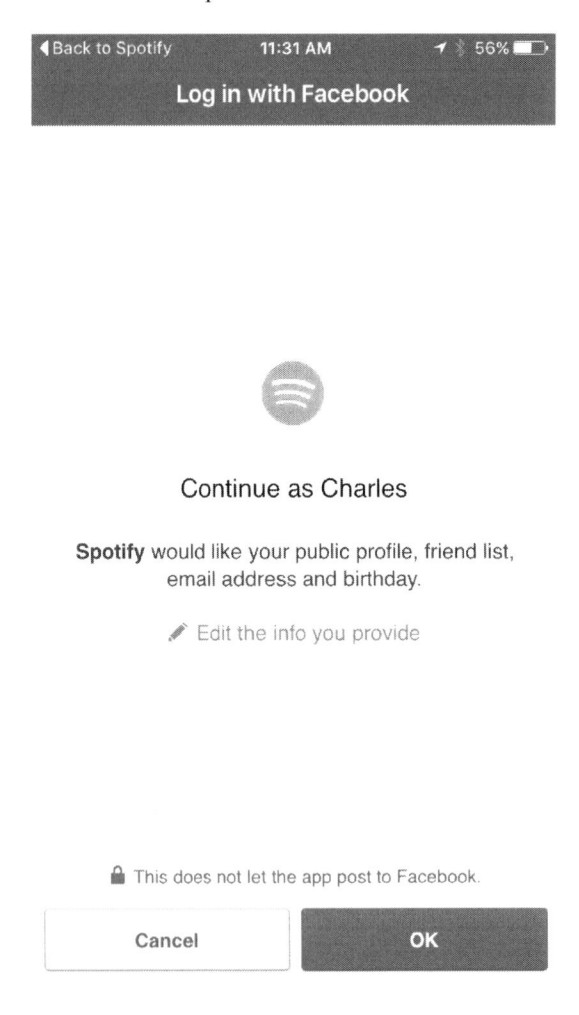

Most major service providers allow you to integrate with their mobile applications in this manner. Doing this provides a more seamless user experience. In addition, this workflow makes use of the existing active session that your user has with that service provider within their mobile application, removing one less request to log in and authorize.

Summary

In this chapter, we have taken a dedicated look at special considerations for integrating with OAuth 2.0 service providers via native mobile applications. We explored the appropriate flow to use from native mobile applications, as well as alternatives that make use of certain platforms' capabilities. There are very important, but subtle, security implications that are important for developers to be aware of. We then discussed how to leverage both workflows in a hybrid architecture to maximize performance and security. Finally, we looked at special provisions that are allowed to mobile application developers integrating with certain major service providers. In the next chapter, we will look at how to troubleshoot your OAuth 2.0 application in an effective and efficient manner.

11
Tooling and Troubleshooting

At this point in the book, we have covered everything you need to know to integrate with any OAuth 2.0-compliant service provider. But even under ideal conditions, you're bound to run into some issues. This chapter is dedicated to helping you identify and solve those issues. We will look at various tips and techniques you can use to troubleshoot your application. We will also look at common tools that you should familiarize yourself with to become proficient in dealing with OAuth 2.0 flows.

Tools

Before we dive into troubleshooting, it would be beneficial to explore the tools we will be using. Fortunately for us, the toolset required for effectively troubleshooting an OAuth 2.0 workflow is quite simple and widely available. We will primarily be using two tools to troubleshoot our flows. They are:

- A modern web browser, such as Chrome, Firefox, or Edge
- cURL, the command-line utility

That's it! With these two tools in your arsenal, you are equipped to effectively troubleshoot any OAuth 2.0 workflow.

> **What is cURL?**
>
> **cURL** (pronounced as it is spelled, "curl") is a command-line utility for transferring data and making HTTP requests. It is provided natively in most Linux/Unix-based operating systems, including Mac OS X. There is support for it on Windows, but must be installed manually.
>
> It is a great utility for testing OAuth 2.0 workflows as you can use it to simulate many of the requests that your application will make, but you can do so via simple command-line commands rather than programming them into your application. Getting comfortable with cURL will benefit you greatly as you work with the OAuth 2.0 protocol.

Troubleshooting

As we've discovered throughout the book, the OAuth 2.0 protocol is simply a series of structured HTTP requests and responses to facilitate the transfer of data. Because of the straightforward nature of the protocol, we are able to troubleshoot issues with basic tools. In fact, we can simulate the majority of our implemented OAuth 2.0 flows with these tools alone, separate from our application. Here is the approach we will take:

- If it's a `POST` request, we can simulate it with a cURL command
- If it's a `GET` request, we can simulate it directly within our browser, or with a cURL command

With this approach in mind, we can now look at the various flows that we've examined in the book, this time, simulating them with our tools instead of within our application. Let's begin!

The implicit grant flow

The purpose of the implicit grant flow is to gain authorization from the user in the form of an access token from the service provider. It begins with the authorization request.

The authorization request

When operating without the presence of a backend server, simulating this flow outside of our application is quite easy. Recall that the authorization request is simply a `GET` request to the service provider's authorization endpoint, of the form:

```
GET /authorize?
   response_type=token&
   client_id=[CLIENT_ID]&
   redirect_uri=[REDIRECT_URI]&
   scope=[SCOPE]&
   state=[STATE] HTTP/1.1
Host: server.example.com
```

To simulate this, simply construct your authorization request as outlined earlier, and navigate to it directly in your web browser. If you've constructed this correctly, you should see the user consent screen that will be presented to your users:

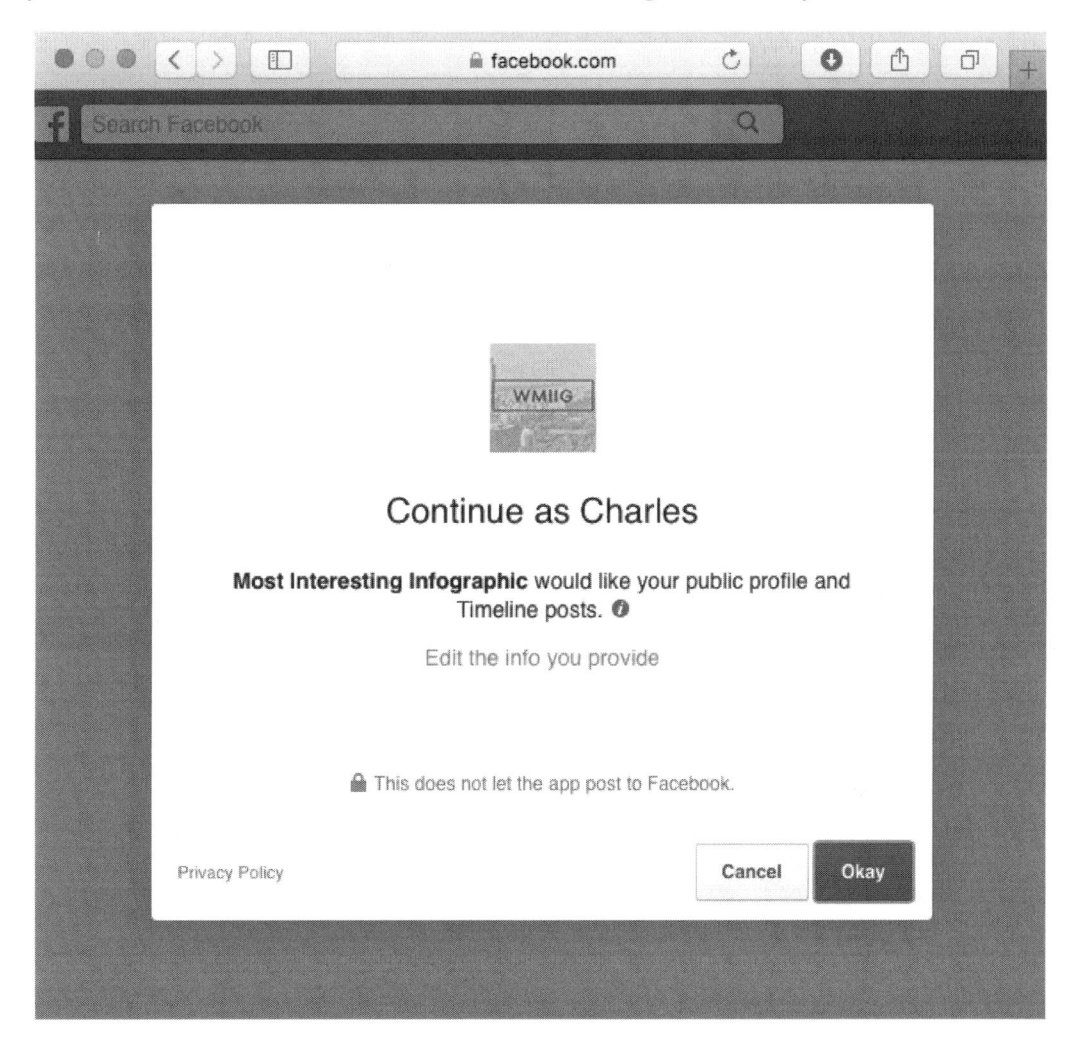

From here, you can accept or deny the request. Doing this will redirect you back to your redirection endpoint. If you have your application running, you can debug directly into your callback handler. Otherwise, your page will error while attempting to load your redirection endpoint. However, the endpoint will be available for you to examine in the URL bar of your browser:

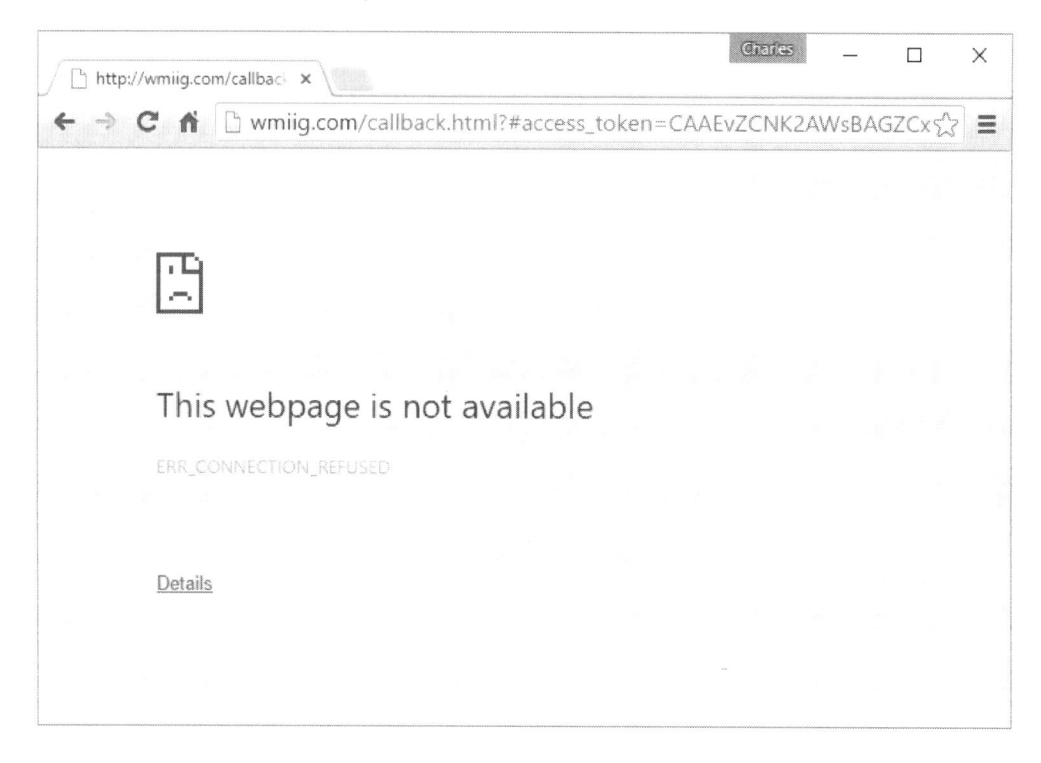

You can extract this response URL and examine it. It should either contain an access token in the case of success, or an error otherwise.

Common issues

Common issues, and suggested troubleshooting approaches, are:

- The user consent screen is not displayed

    It's possible that your authorization endpoint is incorrect. Verify that the authorization endpoint for your service provider is correct.

- Once your user authorizes, you get redirected back to the wrong redirect URI

    You may be specifying your redirect URI incorrectly in your request. Make sure your redirect URI is specified correctly in your initial request by inspecting the `redirect_uri` parameter.

- Getting an authorization code instead of an access token

    You've likely used the wrong response type for your authorization request. Examine your initial authorization request and ensure that your `response_type` parameter is set to `token` and not `code`.

The authorization code grant flow

Just as with the implicit grant flow, the purpose of the authorization code grant flow is to obtain authorization from the user in the form of an access token from the service provider. It begins with an authorization request for an authorization code followed by an access token request for an access token.

The authorization request

Similar to the authorization request of the implicit grant flow, the authorization request for the authorization code grant flow is simply a GET request to the service provider's authorization endpoint, of the form:

```
GET /authorize?
    response_type=code&
    client_id=[CLIENT_ID]&
    redirect_uri=[REDIRECT_URI]&
    scope=[SCOPE]&
    state=[STATE] HTTP/1.1
Host: server.example.com
```

This can be simulated in the browser just as it was done with the authorization request in the preceding implicit grant flow.

Common issues

Common issues, and suggested troubleshooting approaches, are:

- User consent screen doesn't display

    It's possible that your authorization endpoint is incorrect. Verify that the authorization endpoint for your service provider is correct.

- Once your user authorizes, you get redirected back to the wrong redirect URI

  You may be specifying your redirect URI incorrectly in your request. Make sure your redirect URI is specified correctly in your initial request by inspecting the `redirect_uri` parameter.

- Getting an access token instead of an authorization code

  You've likely used the wrong response type for your authorization request. Examine your initial authorization request and ensure that your `response_type` parameter is set to `code` and not `token`.

The access token request

Once you've successfully made your authorization request, you should have gained an authorization code (either via the redirection endpoint in your running application, or pulled directly from the browser URL). Now, you must exchange this for an access token. This is done with a POST request, of the form:

```
POST /token HTTP/1.1
Host: server.example.com
Authorization: Basic [ENCODED_CLIENT_CREDENTIALS]
Content-Type: application/x-www-form-urlencoded

grant_type=authorization_code&
    code=[AUTHORIZATION_CODE]&
    redirect_uri=[REDIRECT_URI]&
    client_id=[CLIENT_ID]
```

Since this is a POST request, we cannot simulate this easily in the browser. Rather, we must defer to our cURL utility instead. This can be simulated with a cURL command, like this:

```
curl --request POST
    -u [CLIENT_ID]:[CLIENT_SECRET]
    --data-urlencode "grant_type=authorization_code"
    --data-urlencode "code=[AUTHORIZATION_CODE]"
    --data-urlencode "redirect_uri=[REDIRECT_URI]"
    --data-urlencode "client_id=[CLIENT_ID]"
    [AUTH_ENDPOINT]
```

Executing this cURL command with the authorization code that you received in the previous step should give you output similar to this:

```
> curl -request POST
    -u wmiig-550106:DFIAJAO98SH9832HVMQI3
    --data-urlencode "grant_type=authorization_code"
    --data-urlencode "code=AQCbhXyIGf5TT3b7YmGMz"
    --data-urlencode "redirect_uri=http://wmiig.com/callback.html"
    --data-urlencode "client_id=wmiig-550106"
    https://graph.facebook.com/oauth/access_token
> access_token=CAAEvZCNK2AWsBZDZD&expires=5111724
```

Common issues

Common issues, and suggested troubleshooting approaches, are as follows:

- Unable to exchange authorization code for access token

    Remember that authorization codes are consumable. Make sure that you are not attempting to use an authorization code more than once to get an access token.

    Authorization codes also typically have a short lifetime. The OAuth 2.0 specification actually recommends the maximum lifetime for an authorization code to be 10 minutes. If you've waited longer than 10 minutes to use your authorization code, it is likely expired. Fetch a new one and try again.

The API call flow

At this point, you should have a valid access token and you would like to make an API call to access a protected resource. Recall from *Chapter 7, Use Your Access Token* that there are three methods available to use to pass your access token in an API call. Let's look at how we can simulate all three of these methods for the purpose of testing and debugging.

The authorization request header field

To pass your access token via the authorization request header field, you must add the Authorization header to your GET request, like this:

```
GET /resource HTTP/1.1
Host: server.example.com
Authorization: Bearer mF_9.B5f-4.1JqM
```

Tooling and Troubleshooting

Since this requires the modification of request headers, this cannot be simulated in the browser. However, this can easily be simulated via a simple cURL command:

`curl -H "Authorization: Bearer [ACCESS_TOKEN]" http://www.example.com`

Let's see what this command looks like when requesting access to the user resource in the Facebook Graph API:

```
> curl -H "Authorization: Bearer CAAEvZCNK2AWsBZDZD"
    https://graph.facebook.com/v2.5/me?fields=name
> {"name":"John Smith","id":"1012877671"}
```

Common issues

Common issues, and suggested troubleshooting approaches, are as follows:

- Access denied

    The scope for the access token you are using does not cover the protected resource you are trying to access. Perhaps you are using an access token for a scope other than the scope that was granted in your original authorization request. Modify your scope in the initial authorization request and try again.

The form-encoded body parameter

To pass your access token via the form-encoded body parameter method, you must make a `POST` request specifying the appropriate parameters within the request body encoded according to the `application/x-www-form-urlencoded` format, like this:

```
POST /resource HTTP/1.1
Host: server.example.com
Content-Type: application/x-www-form-urlencoded

access_token=mF_9.B5f-4.1JqM
```

Since this is a `POST` request, we can simulate this with a cURL request:

```
curl --request POST
    --data-urlencode "access_token=[ACCESS_TOKEN]"
    --data-urlencode "method=get"
    http://www.example.com
```

Once again, doing this with the user API, we get a result similar to this:

```
> curl --request POST
    --data-urlencode "access_token=CAAEvZCNK2wZDZD"
    --data-urlencode "method=get"
    https://graph.facebook.com/v2.5/me?fields=name
> {"name":"John Smith","id":"1012877671"}
```

Common issues

Common issues, and suggested troubleshooting approaches, are as follows:

- Getting a blank or "success" response without the actual data

    Since we are making a POST request, some service providers respect RESTful API architectures and take this to be an update request. They may require you to specify the type of request explicitly as we have done above with the parameter `method=get`. Refer to your service provider's documentation to see if such a parameter is required for your API calls as well.

The URI query parameter

This final method for passing in your access token requires that you simply append it as a parameter to the end of your access request:

```
GET /resource?access_token=mF_9.B5f-4.1JqM HTTP/1.1
Host: server.example.com
```

Since this is a GET request, we can simulate this very simply by plugging this directly into a browser and observing the results:

If you wish to do this with cURL as well, you can. Simply execute the command using the form:

```
curl "https://server.example.com?access_token=[ACCESS_TOKEN]"
```

Executing this against the user API, we get output similar to the following:

```
> curl "https://graph.facebook.com/v2.5/me?fields=name&access_token=CAAEvZCNK2A"
> {"name":"Charles Bihis","id":"1123581321345589"}
```

After demonstrating the simplicity of this method for passing your access token, it is easy to see why this is the preferred method to use when testing and debugging your application. You can easily test whether your API calls are well-formed, or your access tokens are still valid, using this method. However, once you move to a production setting, you should abandon this method and move to one of the other two, more secure, methodologies.

The refresh token flow

The refresh token flow is used to gain a new, valid, access token in case your old one has expired. Recall from *Chapter 8, Refresh Your Access Token*, this is done with a POST request to the service provider's token endpoint, with the following form:

```
POST /token HTTP/1.1
Host: server.example.com
Authorization: Basic [ENCODED_CLIENT_CREDENTIALS]
Content-Type: application/x-www-form-urlencoded

grant_type=refresh_token&refresh_token=[REFRESH_TOKEN]
```

This is similar to the access token request in the authorization code grant flow, and so the cURL command is similar as well:

```
curl --request POST
    -u [CLIENT_ID]:[CLIENT_SECRET]
    --data-urlencode "grant_type=refresh_token"
    --data-urlencode "refresh_token=[REFRESH_TOKEN]"
    [TOKEN_ENDPOINT]
```

Executing this cURL command with a valid refresh token should give you an output similar to this:

```
> curl –request POST
    -u wmiig-550106:DFIAJAO98SH9832HVMQI3
    --data-urlencode "grant_type=refresh_token"
    --data-urlencode "refresh_token=XyIGf5TAQCbhT3b7YmGMz"
    https://graph.facebook.com/oauth/access_token
> access_token=CAAEvZCNK2AWsBZDZD&expires=5111724
```

> **Just an example**
>
> Recall that Facebook doesn't support the refresh token flow. The preceding example is simulated for demonstration purposes.

Common issues

Common issues, and suggested troubleshooting approaches, are as follows:

- No refresh token

    Make sure you are using the authorization code grant flow. The ability to refresh your access token is only available for this flow. Refresh tokens aren't actually returned at all with implicit grant flows.

- An invalid token

    Refresh tokens expire too! They likely have a longer expiry time than access tokens, but they still expire too. If this happens, you must start the whole authorization flow again, possibly requiring the user to re-authenticate.

Summary

We covered some important topics in this chapter. Particularly, we looked at the two most common and useful tools that you, as an application developer, will use to troubleshoot your OAuth 2.0 workflows: the web browser and the cURL command-line utility. We then examined the various OAuth 2.0 flows that we've discussed in the book, replicating their flows manually with the tools we introduced earlier. Doing this outside of our application gives us great introspection into the success (or failure) of our requests without confusing them with issues related to our application. Following this template for validating your flows will help you isolate issues with your OAuth 2.0 requests and will certainly make your integrations less troublesome.

12
Extensions to OAuth 2.0

You finally made it! Welcome to the final chapter of the book. Up until this point, we have discussed all that you need to know to integrate with practically any OAuth 2.0-compliant service provider out there. We examined the protocol, including the process of registration, getting your access token, using your access token, and refreshing your access token. We examined this in the context of an application developer looking to integrate with an OAuth 2.0-compliant service provider via a client-side workflow or server-side workflow, or both. However, OAuth 2.0 has the ability to be extended in various ways, greatly increasing the power and range of applications to which it can be applied.

Extensions to the OAuth 2.0 framework

Throughout the book, we discussed how to integrate with OAuth 2.0-compliant service providers via either the implicit grant flow or the authorization code grant flow. We invoked these flows to request, and subsequently use, access tokens. These flows represent the majority of flows that application developers will encounter. However, this is only a narrow view with regard to the broader range of capabilities allowed by the framework. There are many extensions that can be added to the OAuth 2.0 Authorization Framework to facilitate many additional use cases. Let's take a look at some.

Custom grant types

When your client application interacts with a service provider, such as Facebook, it does so via a particular, predefined grant type. In the book, we discussed the two most commonly used grant types:

- Authorization code grant
- Implicit grant

However, there are two additional grant types that are supported:

- Resource owner password credentials grant
- Client credentials grant

These are less commonly supported by consumer service providers, such as Google and Facebook, and so we chose to omit detailed discussions of those within the main content of the book. However, if you would like to learn more about these protocols, you can read more about them in the appendices (*Appendix A, Resource Owner Password Credentials Grant* and *Appendix B, Client Credentials Grant*).

In addition to natively supporting these four grant types, the OAuth 2.0 framework allows for the specification of additional custom grant types. These will be determined and implemented by the service provider. So, perhaps your workplace decides to use OAuth 2.0 to restrict access to certain parts of your company's data, but your IT team and security team do not want to use any of the four natively supported grant flows. They can, instead, design and implement their own grant type, which your client application will subsequently use to request access tokens and access those protected resources.

A variety of token types

Once a grant type is decided, your client application will interact with a service provider through the exchange of tokens. Once your user authenticates and authorizes your application, they are given a bearer token, which your application can then use to access a protected resource on their behalf. The properties of these tokens are quite loosely defined, described by the specification simply as opaque string values that encapsulate an authentication for a particular user. They can simply be unique strings that match up with a set of permissions for a user. Many service providers implement their tokens in this non-standard, custom way. However, it is useful to know that there are two popular token formats that can be used by service providers, if desired:

- JSON Web Tokens (JWT)
- SAML assertions

Both of these token formats describe a standard for the creation and use of security tokens. These tokens are known as security tokens because they make use of cryptography to facilitate features that would not normally be allowed via simple opaque string values.

JWTs are most commonly seen in the consumer space (they are used in the OpenID Connect protocol, which we will explore later). Compared with SAML assertions, JWTs can be considered a simpler version of security token than a SAML assertion, with a simpler format and encoding syntax. SAML assertions, on the other hand, employ a standard for security tokens that is more expressive and powerful than JWTs, at the cost of added complexity. These will typically be seen in the enterprise space where SAML integration for authentication is more prevalent.

Both of these formats can act as bearer tokens in the OAuth 2.0 protocol, as long as they are supported by the service provider.

Any authorization backend

One of the major benefits of the OAuth 2.0 protocol is that it has the ability to encapsulate and abstract away the authentication layer of a service, wrapping it with a standard, uniform layer for client applications to consume. For instance, your company may be using a Kerberos-based authentication system, say LDAP, for your company's internal authentication. They may, at some point, choose to wrap this with an OAuth 2.0 layer, which would effectively encapsulate their authentication layer and present a uniform interface to any interested parties. Now, they can change their internal authentication methodologies, say, to SAML, and clients would be largely unaware (they may be presented a different user consent screen, but other than that, behavior should be largely unaffected).

This is a very powerful concept. Abstracting away the authentication layer provides a uniform interface for clients while maintaining flexibility for the underlying protocols to change without affecting (that is, breaking) clients.

OpenID Connect

The OAuth 2.0 Authorization Framework describes a protocol for managing authorization to protected resources for your service. It does not, however, describe methods for authentication. OpenID Connect is a protocol built on top of the OAuth 2.0 protocol in order to provide a complete solution for both authentication and authorization. In short, OpenID Connect provides an identity layer on top of the authorization protocol described by OAuth 2.0. This allows client applications to verify the identity of an end-user based on the authentication performed while gaining user consent. Most importantly, this can all be done by the client application without having to store or manage passwords.

Extensions to OAuth 2.0

You may recall from *Chapter 1, Why Should I Care About OAuth 2.0?* that we introduced the concepts of federated identity and delegated authority and mentioned that they are actually the same underlying concept. In one delegated authority scenario, the user is delegating authority for a client application to access some protected resource on their behalf, say, access to their Facebook friend list. However, this protected resource can be anything. It can even be their profile information as stored by Facebook. Delegating access to this resource gives the client application the means of verifying the end-user's identity without ever seeing their credentials.

Let's see how this is accomplished with OpenID Connect using a familiar OAuth 2.0 workflow. What follows is a modified version of the authorization code grant flow that we explored in *Chapter 6, Get an Access Token with the Server-Side Flow*:

1. The client application initiates the authorization request using the authorization code grant flow. However, in this authorization request, a subset of the following OpenID Connect scopes is requested:
    - `openid`: (Required) This indicates to the service provider that the client is making an OpenID Connect request
    - `profile`: (Optional) This requests access to the user's profile information
    - `email`: (Optional) This requests access to the user's e-mail address
    - `address`: (Optional) This requests access to the user's address information
    - `phone`: (Optional) This requests access to the user's phone number
2. The user is presented with the same user consent screen that we are familiar with. If they accept, they are redirected back to the application via the redirection endpoint, passing along with it the corresponding authorization code.
3. The client application will take this authorization code and make a request to the service provider's token endpoint to exchange it for an access token.
4. The response from this request will contain an access token (as the property `access_token`). However, it will contain an additional token known as an ID token (as the property `id_token`). This ID token is not a bearer token as the access token is, but rather, it is a JSON Web Token.
5. The client application then validates the ID token and obtains the user's profile information.

As you can see, this flow is very similar to the authorization code grant flow we learned earlier, except now we are able to verify the identity of the user, something we were unable to do with OAuth 2.0 alone. A deeper discussion of OpenID Connect is outside the scope of this book, but I encourage you to explore it on your own as it is an elegant solution for providing a full end-to-end authentication and authorization solution. And just like OAuth 2.0, it is quickly gaining adoption. You can read more about OpenID Connect by visiting their website, currently located at `http://openid.net/connect/`.

Summary

In this chapter, we concluded our discussion of the OAuth 2.0 protocol by looking at the various ways it can be extended and customized to meet the needs of almost any situation. With such extensibility, the protocol gains flexibility and robustness, allowing it to be used in a multitude of scenarios. You will typically see it in a consumer setting offered to third-party developers, such as yourselves, by service providers such as Facebook, Google, and Instagram. In addition to exploring the ways that OAuth 2.0 can be extended, we took a dedicated look at a particular extension in OpenID Connect. We examined a basic OpenID Connect flow to gain profile information about the user, and demonstrated that it is actually very similar to the authorization code grant flow we explored in *Chapter 6, Get an Access Token with the Server-Side Flow*.

Because of the amazing flexibility that OAuth 2.0 provides, many businesses and enterprises are adopting it as an authorization layer internally, encapsulating their internal enterprise systems. The prevalence of OAuth 2.0 is quite established, and is only growing. Now, you have the tools to comfortably integrate with the most common and powerful authorization framework in the world! Now, go and build the next great application!

A
Resource Owner Password Credentials Grant

The resource owner password credentials grant is an additional grant type supported by the OAuth 2.0 specification. It isn't commonly used or supported by service providers due to its low level of security. In a nutshell, this grant type operates by utilizing the user's actual credentials to gain an access token. This is in stark contrast to the other grant types, where the client application is completely unaware of the user's credentials. However, in this grant type, users send their credentials to the client application to use on their behalf to access protected resources.

Once the client application has a user's credentials, it uses them to gain an access token, just as in the other grant types. In this sense, risk is mitigated slightly, compared to using the credentials directly, since tokens have limited scope and duration (unlike passwords). However, the passing and delegation of user credentials is highly undesirable due to the risk of leaking this important information.

When should you use it?

Due to the high level of risk associated with this grant type, it should only be used when both the authorization code grant and implicit grant are unavailable. This grant type is well-suited for migrating existing clients using direct authentication schemes such as HTTP basic or digest authentication to an OAuth 2.0 flow since it makes use of the same stored credentials that those legacy authentication methods use.

Reference pages

Use these pages as reference documentation when implementing the password credentials grant flow in your application. Adapted from *The OAuth 2.0 Authorization Framework* specification [RFC 6749].

An overview of the resource owner password credentials grant

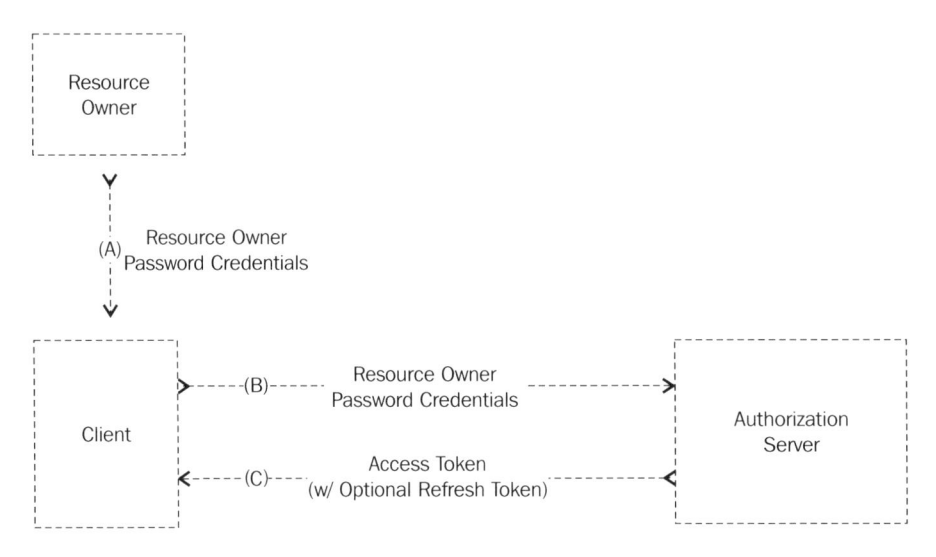

Figure 5 from RFC 6749

The steps are as follows:

- **A**: The user provides the client application with their username and password.
- **B**: The client requests an access token from the service provider's token endpoint using the credentials received from the user. During this step, the client application authenticates with the service provider as well.
- **C**: The service provider authenticates the client and validates the user credentials received, and if valid, issues an access token.

Authorization request and response

The method through which the client obtains the user's credentials is beyond the scope of the specification. Once an access token has been obtained, these credentials must then be discarded.

Access token request

The client makes a `POST` request to the service provider's token endpoint passing in the following parameters encoded using the `application/x-www-form-urlencoded` format as described in Appendix B of the specification:

- `grant_type`: (Required) This is the value that must be set to `password`
- `username`: (Required) This is the user's username
- `password`: (Required) This is the user's password
- `scope`: (Optional) A list of space-delimited, case-sensitive strings which represent the scope of the access request

As part of this request, the client application must also authenticate with the service provider. This is typically done using the HTTP basic authentication scheme [RFC 2617], but other authentication schemes may be supported by the service provider as well, such as HTTP digest authentication or public/private key authentication

An example access token request using HTTP basic authentication looks like:

```
POST /token HTTP/1.1
Host: server.example.com
Authorization: Basic czZCaGRSa3F0MzpnWDFmQmF0M2JW
Content-Type: application/x-www-form-urlencoded

grant_type=password&username=johndoe&password=A3ddj3w
```

Access token response

If the access token request is valid and authorized, the response will contain an access token, an optional refresh token, and other parameters, described as follows:

- `access_token`: (Required) The access token issued by the service provider.
- `token_type`: (Required) The type of the token issued. This value is case-insensitive.
- `expires_in`: (Optional) The lifetime of the access token given in seconds. If omitted, the service provider should communicate the expiration time via other means.
- `refresh_token`: (Optional) A refresh token, which can be used to obtain new access tokens using the refresh token workflow.
- `scope`: (Conditionally required) A list of space-delimited, case-sensitive strings which represent the scope of the access granted. Required only if the scope granted is different from the scope requested.

An example access token response looks like this:

```
HTTP/1.1 200 OK
Content-Type: application/json;charset=UTF-8
Cache-Control: no-store
Pragma: no-cache

{
  "access_token":"2YotnFZFEjr1zCsicMWpAA",
  "token_type":"bearer",
  "expires_in":3600,
  "refresh_token":"tGzv3JOkF0XG5Qx2TlKWIA",
  "example_parameter":"example_value"
}
```

Error response

If the access token request fails for any reason, the server will respond with an HTTP 400 (Bad Request) status code including the following properties:

- `error`: (Required) This is a single error code representing the condition that caused the request to fail. The value must be one of the following:

- ○ `invalid_request`: The request is missing a required parameter, includes an unsupported parameter value (other than the grant type), repeats a parameter, includes multiple credentials, utilizes more than one mechanism for authenticating the client, or is otherwise malformed.
- ○ `invalid_client`: The client authentication failed for some reason (for example, an unknown client, no client authentication included, or an unsupported authentication method).
- ○ `invalid_grant`: The provided authorization grant or the refresh token is invalid, expired, revoked, does not match the redirection URI used in the authorization request, or was issued to another client.
- ○ `unauthorized_client`: The authenticated client is not authorized to use this authorization grant type.
- ○ `unsupported_grant_type`: The authorization grant type is not supported by the authorization server.
- ○ `invalid_scope`: The requested scope is invalid, unknown, malformed, or exceeds the scope granted by the user.
- `error_description`: (Optional) Human-readable ASCII message providing additional information regarding the error.
- `error_uri`: (Optional) A URI identifying a human-readable web page providing additional information regarding the error.

An example error response looks like this:

```
HTTP/1.1 400 Bad Request
Content-Type: application/json;charset=UTF-8
Cache-Control: no-store
Pragma: no-cache

{
  "error":"invalid_request"
}
```

B
Client Credentials Grant

The client credentials grant is an additional grant type supported by the OAuth 2.0 specification. This grant type is focused on gaining an access token on behalf of the client application. This is unlike the other three workflows defined by the specification (the authorization code grant, the implicit grant, and the resource owner password credentials grant) in that those flows request access tokens on behalf of a user.

When should you use it?

There may be occasions where your client application has resources with a service provider that are owned and consumed by the client application itself, and not by an end-user. For instance, you may be developing a client application that uses Google Cloud SQL to persist its own application data (as opposed to a user's data). In this case, the client credentials grant is ideal. With this workflow, your client application can request an access token on its own behalf, and then subsequently use that access token to access the protected resources it needs. In the case of our example, the client application would use the client credentials grant flow to authenticate its calls to the Google Cloud SQL APIs. No user intervention is required, and no additional risk is exposed.

Reference pages

Use these pages as reference documentation when implementing the client credentials grant flow in your application. Adapted from *The OAuth 2.0 Authorization Framework* specification [RFC 6749].

Overview of the client credentials grant

```
                >-(A)-- Client Authentication ----->
        Client                                         Authorization
                <-(B)------ Access Token ---------<    Server
```

Figure 6 from RFC 6749

The steps are as follows:

- **A**: The client authenticates with the service provider and requests an access token from the service provider's token endpoint.
- **B**: The service provider authenticates the client, and if valid, issues an access token.

Authorization request and response

Since the client is requesting on their own behalf, no further authorization is needed.

Access token request

The client makes a `POST` request to the service provider's token endpoint passing in the following parameters encoded using the `application/x-www-form-urlencoded` format, as described in Appendix B of the specification:

- `grant_type`: (Required) The value must be set to `client_credentials`
- `scope`: (Optional) A list of space-delimited, case-sensitive strings that represent the scope of the access request

As part of this request, the client application must also authenticate with the service provider. This is typically done using the HTTP basic authentication scheme [RFC 2617], but other authentication schemes may be supported by the service provider as well, such as HTTP digest authentication or public/private key authentication.

An example access token request using HTTP basic authentication looks like:

```
POST /token HTTP/1.1
Host: server.example.com
Authorization: Basic czZCaGRSa3F0MzpnWDFmQmF0M2JW
Content-Type: application/x-www-form-urlencoded

grant_type=client_credentials
```

Access token response

If the access token request is valid and authorized, the response will contain an access token, an optional refresh token, and other parameters, as described here:

- `access_token`: (Required) The access token issued by the service provider.
- `token_type`: (Required) The type of the token issued. This value is case-insensitive.
- `expires_in`: (Optional) The lifetime of the access token given in seconds. If omitted, the service provider should communicate the expiration time via other means.
- `refresh_token`: (Optional) A refresh token, which can be used to obtain new access tokens using the refresh token workflow.
- `scope`: (Conditionally required) A list of space-delimited, case-sensitive strings that represent the scope of the access granted. Required only if the scope granted is different from the scope requested.

An example access token response looks like this:

```
HTTP/1.1 200 OK
Content-Type: application/json;charset=UTF-8
Cache-Control: no-store
Pragma: no-cache

{
  "access_token":"2YotnFZFEjr1zCsicMWpAA",
  "token_type":"bearer",
  "expires_in":3600,
  "refresh_token":"tGzv3JOkF0XG5Qx2TlKWIA",
  "example_parameter":"example_value"
}
```

Error response

If the access token request fails for any reason, the server will respond with an HTTP 400 (Bad Request) status code including the following properties:

- `error`: (Required) This is a single error code representing the condition that caused the request to fail. The value must be one of the following:
    - `invalid_request`: The request is missing a required parameter, includes an unsupported parameter value (other than the grant type), repeats a parameter, includes multiple credentials, utilizes more than one mechanism for authenticating the client, or is otherwise malformed.
    - `invalid_client`: Client authentication failed for some reason (for example, unknown client, no client authentication included, or unsupported authentication method).
    - `invalid_grant`: The provided authorization grant or refresh token is invalid, expired, revoked, does not match the redirection URI used in the authorization request, or was issued to another client.
    - `unauthorized_client`: The authenticated client is not authorized to use this authorization grant type.
    - `unsupported_grant_type`: The authorization grant type is not supported by the authorization server.
    - `invalid_scope`: The requested scope is invalid, unknown, malformed, or exceeds the scope granted by the resource owner.
- `error_description`: (Optional) Human-readable ASCII message providing additional information regarding the error.
- `error_uri`: (Optional) A URI identifying a human-readable web page providing additional information regarding the error.

An example error response looks like this:

```
HTTP/1.1 400 Bad Request
Content-Type: application/json;charset=UTF-8
Cache-Control: no-store
Pragma: no-cache

{
  "error":"invalid_request"
}
```

C
Reference Specifications

The following is a list of important specifications relating to the OAuth 2.0 protocol.

The OAuth 2 Authorization Framework

https://tools.ietf.org/html/rfc6749

This is the specification for the OAuth 2.0 protocol that we have been working with for the duration of the book. Refer to this for more information that was not covered in the main body of the text.

The OAuth 2 Authorization Framework: Bearer Token Usage

https://tools.ietf.org/html/rfc6750

This specification defines the usage protocol for the bearer tokens issued by service providers and used by client applications.

OAuth 2.0 Token Revocation

https://tools.ietf.org/html/rfc7009

This document details the proposal for an additional endpoint for the purpose of revoking previously issued tokens.

OAuth 2.0 Thread Model and Security Considerations

https://tools.ietf.org/html/rfc6819
This document presents a thorough threat model for the OAuth 2.0 protocol.

Assertion Framework for OAuth 2.0 Client Authentication and Authorization Grants

http://tools.ietf.org/html/rfc7521
This specification documents the use of assertions with the OAuth 2.0 protocol in the form of a new client authentication mechanism and a new authorization grant type.

Security Assertion Markup Language (SAML) 2.0 Profile for OAuth 2.0 Client Authentication and Authorization Grants

https://tools.ietf.org/html/rfc7522
This specification defines the use of a **Security Assertion Markup Language (SAML)** 2.0 assertion for client authentication, as well as for requesting an access token.

JSON Web Token (JWT)

http://tools.ietf.org/html/rfc7519
This document outlines the format for **JSON Web Tokens (JWTs)** as a means of exchanging claims between parties.

JSON Web Token (JWT) Profile for OAuth 2.0 Client Authentication and Authorization Grants

http://tools.ietf.org/html/rfc7523

This specification describes the use of JSON Web Tokens (JWTs) as a means of client authentication, as well as for requesting an access token.

OpenID Connect Core 1.0

http://openid.net/specs/openid-connect-core-1_0.html

This document outlines the OpenID Connect protocol, which is a protocol built on top of the OAuth 2.0 protocol to provide a full end-to-end authentication and authorization framework.

HTTP Authentication: Basic and Digest Access Authentication

https://www.ietf.org/rfc/rfc2617

This specification outlines the authentication methods used for passing client credentials and access tokens using the authorization request header field to the service provider.

Index

A

access token
  about 20, 119
  access duration 41
  authorization request header
    field, defining 120, 121
  defining 39, 43
  form-encoded body parameter, using 121
  obtaining 38, 39
  refreshing 43
  scope 39-41
  token revocation 41
  URI query parameter, using 121, 122
  used, for creating API call 120
  using 42
  versus bearer token 20
access token request
  about 91
  according, to specification 91-93
  defining 198, 199
  in application 93
  making 106, 107
access token response
  about 94, 137
  defining 60, 199
  error 62, 95, 138, 139
  handling 73-77, 108, 111
  parameters 61, 144
  properties 80
  success 60-62, 94, 95, 137, 138
Apache Maven
  defining 64
  installing 96, 97
  URL 64

API call
  creating, access token used 120
API call flow
  about 179
  authorization request header field 179
  authorization request header
    field, troubleshooting 180
  common issues, with authorization request
    header field 180
  common issues, with form-encoded body
    parameter 181
  form-encoded body parameter 180
  form-encoded body parameter,
    troubleshooting 181
  URI query parameter, using 181, 182
application
  creating 46-48
  redirection endpoint, setting 48
  registering, with Facebook 46
  service providers authorization, finding 53
  token endpoints, finding 53
auth endpoint
  URL 53
authentication
  about 2
  versus authorization 2
authorization
  about 2
  performing, via mobile application 169, 170
  versus authentication 2
authorization code 26
authorization code grant flow
  about 83-86, 177
  access token request 91, 178, 179
  access token request, troubleshooting 179

[205]

access token response 94
authorization request 86, 177
authorization request, troubleshooting 177
authorization response 88
common issues, with access
    token request 179
common issues, with authorization
    request 177
authorization endpoint
  URL 37
authorization request
  about 86
  according, to specification 86
  creating 71-73
  defining 58
  defining, according to specification 58
  defining, in application 59, 60
  example 79
  in application 87
  making 102-104
  parameters 58
authorization request and response
  defining 198
authorization response
  about 88
  error 89, 90
  handling 104-106
  success 88, 89
auth process
  cons 140
  pros 140

B

base application
  Apache Maven, installing 64
  base project, configuring 67, 68
  building 64, 96
  hosts file, modifying 68, 100
  project, creating 66, 97, 98
  running 68-70, 100-102
base project
  configuring 99, 100
bearer token
  versus access token 20

best practices, security
  authorization code grant
    flow, using 150, 151
  client credentials, rotating 154
  credentials and tokens, maintaining out of
    reach of users 150
  implicit grant flow, using 149, 150
  minimal scopes, requesting 149
  native browsers, using instead of embedded
    browsers 151, 152
  read-only permissions, requesting 149, 150
  refresh token, using 151
  third-party scripts, avoiding in redirection
    endpoint 153, 154
  TLS, using 148, 149

C

client application
  client credentials 38
  different registration process 36, 37
  different service providers 36, 37
  registering 35, 36
  same OAuth 2.0 protocol 36, 37
client credentials grant
  about 197
  defining 198
  reference 198
  using 197
client-side application
  API call, creating 123
  form-encoded body parameter,
    using 125, 126
  GitHub, URL 126
  URI query parameter, using 124
client-side flow
  defining 18
  implicit grant type, using 21, 22
  untrusted client 19-21
common attacks
  about 154
  client and user impersonation 162
  Cross-site request forgery (CSRF) 154, 155
  phishing 158, 159
  redirection URI manipulation 160-162

[206]

Cross-site request forgery (CSRF)
 about 154, 155
 state param used, for combating 156, 157
cURL 173
custom grant types
 about 185, 186
 authorization code grant 185
 implicit grant 185

D

delegated authority 3, 4

E

embedded browser
 versus native browser 152, 153
error, access token response
 parameters 62
error response
 defining 200
 parameters 145
 properties 200
expired refresh token
 defining 43, 139
extensions, OAuth 2.0 framework
 authorization backend 187
 custom grant types 185, 186
 token types 186, 187

F

Facebook
 references 53
Facebook Graph API
 about 122
 URL 122
federated identity 3, 4

G

GoodApp application
 defining 34
 trusted, versus untrusted clients 17, 18
 user consent 13-16
 workflows, defining for clients 16, 17
 working 11-13

H

hybrid architecture
 about 167
 authorization code grant, for backend
  server 168, 169
 benefits 169
 implicit grant flow, for mobile app 168, 169

I

implicit grant flow
 about 174
 access token response 60
 authorization request 58, 174-176
 authorization request,
  troubleshooting 176, 177
 common issues, with authorization
  request 176, 177
 defining 55-57
implicit grant type
 using 22
infographic
 creating 130
 URL 130
installation, Apache Maven 96, 97

J

jQuery library
 URL 154
JSON Web Tokens (JWTs) 202

M

mobile
 defining 18, 30, 51
mobile application
 about 163
 authorization, performing via 169, 170
 considerations 164
 flow type, deciding 164
 security considerations 165-167
 with secure storage APIs, on mobile
  platforms 165

N

native browser
  versus embedded browser 152, 153

O

OAuth 1.0 1
OAuth 2.0
  about 1
  authorization framework 17, 18
  defining 33
  delegated authority 4
  examples, defining 4
  federated identity 3, 4
  trusted 18
  untrusted 18
  used, for solving problem 5
  using 3, 8
OAuth 2.0 framework
  extensions 185
OAuth 2.0 protocol
  reference specifications 201-203
OpenID Connect
  about 187
  URL 189
  using 188, 189

P

perpetual tokens 41
phishing 158, 159
problem solving
  with OAuth 2.0 7, 8
  without OAuth 2.0 5, 6
project object model (POM) 64

R

redirection endpoint
  defining 48-52
  references 52, 53
  URL 37
reference pages
  access token response 80, 144
  defining 78, 143
  error response 80, 81, 145
  implicit grant flow 78
  refresh request 144
  refresh token flow 143, 144
refresh request
  about 136
  parameters 144
  specification, defining 136, 137
refresh token
  about 42, 135
  defining 42
  incapability 43
refresh token flow
  about 182
  access token response 137
  common issues 183
  cons 140
  defining 135
  pros 140
  refresh request 136
  troubleshooting 183
  versus auth process 140
registration process
  defining 45
resource owner password credentials grant
  about 191
  access token request, defining 193
  access token response, defining 194
  authorization request 193
  authorization response 193
  error response 194, 195
  overview 192
  reference 192
  usage 191

S

sample application
  building 96
scope and duration of access 39
security
  best practices 148
  defining 147
Security Assertion Markup Language (SAML) 2.0 202
server-side application
  API call, creating 126
  GitHub, URL 129

   HTTP authorization header, using 128, 129
   URI query parameter, using 126, 127
server-side flow
   defining 23
   trusted client 24-26
   using 28
   workflow, defining 26-28
server-side workflow
   and client-side workflow, comparing 29
SSO (Single Sign On) 73

T

token endpoint
   URL 37
token revocation 41
token types
   about 186, 187
   JSON Web Tokens (JWT) 186
   SAML assertions 186
tools
   using 173
troubleshooting
   about 174
   API call flow 179
   authorization code grant flow 177
   implicit grant flow 174
   refresh token flow 182
trust 16
trusted client
   about 17
   advantages 29
   disadvantages 29

U

untrusted client
   about 17, 22
   advantages 23
   disadvantages 23
user consent 13-16

W

WMIIG
   about 57
   URL 70
workflow
   defining 141, 142

Thank you for buying
Mastering OAuth 2.0

About Packt Publishing

Packt, pronounced 'packed', published its first book, *Mastering phpMyAdmin for Effective MySQL Management*, in April 2004, and subsequently continued to specialize in publishing highly focused books on specific technologies and solutions.

Our books and publications share the experiences of your fellow IT professionals in adapting and customizing today's systems, applications, and frameworks. Our solution-based books give you the knowledge and power to customize the software and technologies you're using to get the job done. Packt books are more specific and less general than the IT books you have seen in the past. Our unique business model allows us to bring you more focused information, giving you more of what you need to know, and less of what you don't.

Packt is a modern yet unique publishing company that focuses on producing quality, cutting-edge books for communities of developers, administrators, and newbies alike. For more information, please visit our website at `www.packtpub.com`.

About Packt Open Source

In 2010, Packt launched two new brands, Packt Open Source and Packt Enterprise, in order to continue its focus on specialization. This book is part of the Packt Open Source brand, home to books published on software built around open source licenses, and offering information to anybody from advanced developers to budding web designers. The Open Source brand also runs Packt's Open Source Royalty Scheme, by which Packt gives a royalty to each open source project about whose software a book is sold.

Writing for Packt

We welcome all inquiries from people who are interested in authoring. Book proposals should be sent to `author@packtpub.com`. If your book idea is still at an early stage and you would like to discuss it first before writing a formal book proposal, then please contact us; one of our commissioning editors will get in touch with you.

We're not just looking for published authors; if you have strong technical skills but no writing experience, our experienced editors can help you develop a writing career, or simply get some additional reward for your expertise.

[PACKT] open source*
PUBLISHING community experience distilled

OAuth 2.0 Identity and Access Management Patterns

ISBN: 978-1-78328-559-4   Paperback: 128 pages

A practical hands-on guide to implementing secure API authorization flow scenarios with OAuth 2.0

1. Build web, client-side, desktop, and server-side secure OAuth 2.0 client applications by utilizing the appropriate grant flow for the given scenario.

2. Get to know the inner workings of OAuth 2.0 and learn how to handle and implement various authorization flows.

3. Explore practical code examples that are executable as standalone applications running on top of Spring MVC.

Open Source Identity Management Patterns and Practices Using OpenAM 10.x

ISBN: 978-1-78216-682-5   Paperback: 116 pages

An intuitive guide to learning OpenAM access management capabilities for web and application servers

1. Learn patterns, practices, and the terminology of Identity Management.

2. Learn how to install OpenAM 10.x.

3. Protect web and application servers using policy agents.

Please check **www.PacktPub.com** for information on our titles

Oracle Identity and Access Manager 11g for Administrators

ISBN: 978-1-84968-268-8   Paperback: 336 pages

Administer Oracle Identity and Access Management: Installation configuration, and day-to-day tasks

1. Full of illustrations, diagrams, and tips with clear step-by-step instructions and real time examples.
2. Understand how to Integrate OIM/OAM with E-Business Suite, Webcenter, Oracle Internet Directory and Active Directory.
3. Learn various techniques for implementing and managing OIM/OAM with illustrative screenshots.

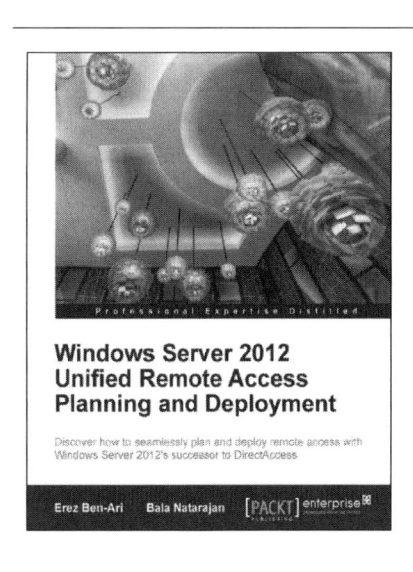

Windows Server 2012 Unified Remote Access Planning and Deployment

ISBN: 978-1-84968-828-4   Paperback: 328 pages

Discover how to seamlessly plan and deploy remote access with Windows Server 2012's successor to DirectAccess

1. The essential administrator's companion for the successor to DirectAccess.
2. Get to grips with configuring, enabling, and deploying Unified Remote Access.
3. A quick start guide to have you up and running with Windows Server 2012 URA in no time.

Please check www.PacktPub.com for information on our titles

Printed in Great Britain
by Amazon